By Nora Scott Kinzer

PUT DOWN AND RIPPED OFF:
The American Woman and the Beauty Cult

STRESS AND
THE AMERICAN WOMAN

Stress and
the American Woman

NORA SCOTT KINZER

1979
Anchor Press/Doubleday
Garden City, New York

Library of Congress Catalog Card Number: 78-1202
ISBN: 0-385-13370-7

This book is dedicated

—to all the people of the world who get up when they don't think it is worth it,

—to every man who finds out that he is not going to realize his potential,

—to every woman whom people describe as "having a lovely personality,"

—to all of us who don't become alcoholics, addicts, or police statistics.

ACKNOWLEDGMENTS

Acknowledgments are either grudgingly given or overly enthusiastic. Mine will be succinct because while many people claim vicarious stress from the writing of this manuscript, I had all the psychosomatic symptoms. The one person responsible for this book is Doubleday's Elizabeth Frost Knappman, who mercilessly hounded me and poked and prodded my reluctant muse. Judy Folkenberg prowled medical libraries and found reams of contradictory data. My faithful secretary, Helen Pahlke, endured my erratic work habits. My bemused and always supportive literary agent, Gerry McCauley, became a therapist listening to an ever-increasing tale of woe. I owe a personal and professional debt to my compatriots and fellow researchers at the United States Military Academy, including Harry Buckley, Allen Vitters, Howard Prince, Theresa Rhone, and Walter Ulmer. Thanks also to my gynecologist, internist, ophthalmologist, and dermatologist, who patched me up under undue stress. Donald Stewart, my beloved husband, suffered through my maladies and procrastinating, insomnia, excuses, and all other malfeasance.

The faults of the book are mine, but so are all the jokes.

CONTENTS

49683

STRESS AND
THE AMERICAN WOMAN

1

What Is Stress?

CHITCHATTING one night at a cocktail party with one of my favorite shrinks, I confessed that I was terribly depressed and very upset, even though I had just moved from a dank, horrible, broken-down house into a spiffy, brand-new home that I had designed and decorated to suit my special tastes. To the tune of tinkling ice cubes and before he moved on to a more interesting group, this psychiatrist looked at me over the rim of his glass and said, "Oh, that's nothing; you're just suffering from moving depression." And off he went, leaving me standing there.

I was furious. I wanted sympathy and he was telling me that I was perfectly normal. I was *only* reacting stressfully to a life change. Instead of getting soothing understanding and chicken soup, I was matter-of-factly dismissed. But he was right. When you move into a lovely new home, get married, start an exciting new job, or finish a long project, you usually get depressed. Or you get the hives, or can't sleep, or suffer a spastic colon, or react in one or more of a thousand other psychosomatic ways. Also, your stomach acts up and your skin breaks out from divorce, death of a close relative, losing your job, or having a serious automobile accident.

Stress is part of living. Stress can kill. Stress is normal. Stress produces abnormal reactions. There's the problem. A dry mouth and a tight stomach before an examination often help a student get good grades. Too many tight stomachs and the student ends up with a bleeding ulcer. Pregnancy involves stress and strain on a woman that *may* lead to a devastating postpartum depression and *may* end up with suicide. Even a Sunday afternoon spent watching an exciting game on TV is stressful, as many Dolphin and Redskin fans know.

At Purdue we used to have grim jokes about the exciting, seesaw Notre Dame-Purdue games. "Wow! That was really a game," we would say, referring to a three-heart-attack game between the two Indiana rivals. Doctors at Purdue had numbers, and many of us knew which numbers designated the cardiac specialists. "Doctor Number Seven. Doctor Number Seven. Please report to the press box," the loudspeakers would call. "Doctor Number Seven" was the hot-shot heart specialist. Once, he was told to report to the press box, where one of the alumni died among the reporters. Even though it was tacky for him to die in a press box filled with cold coffee and half-eaten hot dogs, the sportswriters had good enough taste not to mention it in their Sunday-morning commentaries.

Maybe they should have. Because then the sports fans might have learned that getting riled up over a game and dying over your alma mater indicates a strange priority of values. Or maybe that's going out with a blaze of glory. While the bands play "Hail, Hail, Old Purdue" and the boilermakers thump the bejesus out of those Catholic boys from Notre Dame, you not so peacefully expire. But in the days of Ara Parseghian, it was the Protestant boys from coal towns in Ohio on Notre Dame's Catholic team who thumped the heck out of Purdue. Maybe that was the real stress factor.

Stress was a daily factor in life at Purdue. Therapists flourished in Lafayette. At one time, Lafayette was third in the nation in the per capita ratio of psychiatrists, surpassed only by Topeka, Kansas (home of the Menningers), and Hollywood, California. One night, a psychiatrist friend of mine confessed, "You know, I began my practice here convinced that all the graduate students were paranoids of the first order. The students used to tell me that they were being persecuted, that they couldn't get their theses finished, that each committee member had a different idea of what ought to be included in the final draft, and that committee members fought with each other by pounding on the graduate student. I used to look at them skeptically, write out a prescription for tranquilizers, make another appointment, and shake my head over this large group of unrestrained paranoids.

"But after a couple of years of hearing the *same* stories

from *different* students in *different* faculties with *different* professors, I began to have my doubts. Also, I met some of these very same professors that I had heard about in my patients' sessions, and I heard these men boast about how they tormented their students. That's when I decided that the students were not paranoids but were describing a frightening and terrible reality. Then I prescribed the tranquilizers but only suggested a few sessions to help the students get through their anxiety period. I pointed out to them that they were indeed being persecuted mercilessly.

"Then I attempted to try and help them map out a plan whereby they could make it through graduate school without a spastic colon or a peptic ulcer. Those who survived often paid the price in a broken marriage or in a severely broken spirit. The whole graduate-school syndrome is sick, and I don't see any way that normal young men and women can be expected to survive it intact."

How well I knew the syndrome! My years in graduate school led me to believe that the strong and sane got out early and the others stayed on out of fear or desperation. Most of us knew the kind of toll that we were exacting on our own psyches, bodies, and families. Graduate-student lore revolved around several recurring topics: which professors were relatively easy on their students, how long could one human being survive on four hours of sleep a night, and did Kaopectate really solve graduate-student gut?

Upset stomachs and assorted gastrointestinal problems absorbed us as much as trying to cadge old exams from older, wiser graduate students. Our hands shook from too much coffee, too many cigarettes, too little sleep, and from justifiable paranoia. We *were* being persecuted. Some committed suicide. Pills combined with booze was a favorite method. Another was to run your car ninety miles an hour down the main drag in West Lafayette, driving headlong into a flatiron-shaped bank building situated on a triangle of streets at an intersection at the bottom of a hill. I used to have an account at that bank, and it was particularly disconcerting to notice the constantly boarded-up window that indicated another student had decided that one more rewrite of his or her dissertation simply was not worth it.

It seemed to me then that the majority of the graduate students who were popping pills and attempting suicide were studying social science. They were the ones who should have known better. The ones with the "insight." However, as I found out in later years, engineering and chemistry students were also suffering from institutional stress. There were wife beatings, child abuse, visits to various psychiatrists, divorces. You name it and the graduate school had a corner on the market.

That's not to say that lower-middle-class and blue-collar people do not undergo similar or equally as debilitating stress situations. Of course they do. But I am writing of my own personal experience and those situations garnered from years of counseling and interviews.

In fact, the origins of this book lay in my shock at being told, "Oh you're just suffering from moving depression." As a social scientist and not-so-good therapist, I tried to understand the relationship between stress, disease, psychosomatic illness, and general neurosis. A few years ago, I filled out Holmes and Rahe's Social Readjustment Scale. Using this scale, you get "points" for a number of social-stress situations—whether these are happy or sad is immaterial. My scale was as follows: Divorce (73), Marital separation (65), Personal illness (53), Marital reconciliation (45), Sex difficulties (39), Business readjustment (39), Change in financial status (39), Change to different line of work (36), Mortgage or loan over $10,000 (31), Change in work responsibilities (29), Outstanding personal achievement (28), Change in living conditions (25), Revision of personal habits (24), Trouble with boss (23), Change in work hours, conditions (20), Change in residence (60—since I moved three times), Change in recreational habits (19), Change in social activities (18), Change in sleeping habits (16), Change in number of family gatherings (15), Change in eating habits (15). The grand total of stress points for me at that time in my life was 712! Seven hundred and twelve wild points!

Since Holmes and Rahe devised this scale as an indicator of when and how people got sick in relation to stress situations, it was quite obvious that I was slated for a terrible attack of something. Drs. Holmes and Rahe figured out ranges for their scale. For example, a score *under* 150 meant you had only a 37 per cent chance of a mild illness (like a cold) in the next two years. If your score is between 150 and 300, you have a slightly over 50 per cent chance of getting pneumonia. And if your score is over 300 you have an 80 per cent chance of becoming sick with a serious illness such as cancer or heart attack.

I began to have heart palpitations just thinking about my 712 stress units, or life-change units, as Holmes and Rahe call them. Even though I didn't develop a coronary, I did have two full-blown attacks of pneumonia, weird rashes, churning stomach, and a tied-up gut. My internist and I agreed that all my illnesses were purely psychosomatic, and I drank a lot of Kaopectate. It was just like being back in graduate school. I was driving myself and everyone around me to distraction finishing a book contract, looking for a new job, starting the job, traveling around the country, and mothering four active little boys. Yet things *had* to get done and my body was going to pay a price.

Now let us digress for a moment and discuss the difference between psychosomatic illness and hypochondria. Most people confuse the two. Both psychosomatic illness and hypochondria are "in your head," but one is real and the other imagined. Psychosomatic illness hurts like hell and can kill you. Hypochondria is imagined pain from an imagined source. Both psychosomatic illness and hypochondria can be induced or fostered by physicians. We all know people who doctor-shop, going from physician to physician until they find one who will prescribe the pills they want or perform the operation that they think they need. That's hypochondria. Psychosomatic illness may have a psychological base, but the resulting heart attack, peptic ulcer, bleeding ulcer, or spastic colon is a *physical* reaction. Sometimes removing the patient from a high-pressure job or a rotten marriage will cure the physical symptoms faster than a new tranquilizer.

Many physicians believe that possibly *all* illness has a psychological base. Variations in diet, smoking, or exercise, whether or not the person's culture permits tantrums and crying-and-screaming outbursts—all contribute to differences among cultural or national groups.

That makes a great deal of sense. The body reacts to stress by pumping hormones into action. The body's reaction is essentially the same whether the stress is watching a football game, surviving a frightening accident on the freeway, undergoing childbirth, or running a race. The nervous system goes into play and the pituitary gland answers the alarm system. The pituitary releases adrenocorticotropic hormone (ACTH). The ACTH, in turn, stimulates the adrenal glands, which send out hormones called corticosteroids. The pituitary and adrenal glands work together to balance the body's chemistry and regulate the functions of other organs.

This is an extremely simple explanation of stress reaction. Probably most people are familiar with the biochemical reactions of stress already, since most people have had stress reactions. Sweaty palms, knots in the stomach, cold hands, dry mouth, a little twitch in the eye, or that scary one: chest pains. While various people, various age groups, and various ethnic groups react in differing ways to stress, one thing is common: the *more* worries are masked and withheld the graver the psychosomatic symptoms we suffer.

That's why southern Europeans generally have a lower incidence of heart disease and ulcers than do phlegmatic Wasps. White Anglo-Saxons are taught to behave nicely and not scream, have tantrums, yell, cry, rant, or rave. That's not nice behavior. Greeks yell and Latins scream. That's acceptable behavior. For example, Mediterranean peoples react differently to death and have remarkably dissimilar grieving reactions than do Wasps. A few years ago, my mother-in-law died. One of my Jewish friends came to the funeral. Since this was her first Wasp funeral, she was absolutely shocked.

"You people are completely devoid of any emotion at

all!" she said. "Why, at Jewish funerals the family can get together and moan, cry, and carry on. You just stand around and talk about the weather and how stocks are going up and down. What cold-blooded fish!"

Maybe she was right, but that was the appropriate way for us to behave. Most of the family were embarrassed about having an open casket, but the old lady had insisted on it in her will. For most of us, death was something to deny. You denied it by talking about the weather and stocks going up and down. Periodically I would give a desultory wave at the casket and invite the person I was talking to to "go and have a look, if you want to." It was all perfectly natural. During the funeral, no one cried and no one carried on. We went back to our house and had a few drinks and some food that the neighbors had brought in. And that was that. Because that's the way funerals were supposed to be and that's the proper way for people to behave at funerals. Proper at least if you are a Wasp.

Of course that doesn't mean that the son and the daughter and the grandchildren of the old lady were not grieving. Yes, they were. But they dared not show their emotion in public, because that would be "bad taste." The men of the family were particularly vulnerable and had to keep leaving the room to control their tears and their emotions. If they had been Greek or Italian or Mexican or even Jewish, tears would have been more than appropriate and even expected. No wonder, then, that Wasps end up with heart attacks and ulcers. Hiding the stress reaction and not allowing the stress to have any outlet is like having a poison eating your physical being inside out.

Just as such ethnic groups as Irish, Italian, German, and

Wasp differ from each other, so do individuals within these same groups. Are these differences hereditary? Is there something in the genes that makes some people more immune to stress than others? Why is it that one woman can survive a concentration camp and rebuild and remold her life with determination and stamina, while a middle-class American female goes to pieces when her teen-age daughters start their adolescent rebellion? Are there such things as schizophrenic families? Many researchers think so.

There is much contradictory and even opposing evidence on whether environment or heredity causes disease. Schizophrenia, like heart disease, does run in families. Does that mean that you have a 50 per cent chance of being incarcerated in a mental hospital because your grandfather was institutionalized? Or do people actually *learn* abnormal ways of behaving? No one can be sure.

However, researchers have found that in schizophrenic families one child seems to be "picked out" by the family as the person who will grow up "crazy." More often than not, a disturbed mother chooses the oldest child to be the goat. The mother builds up resentment over her unwanted pregnancy, her morning sickness, and the fact that she gave up her job and correspondingly the family's standard of living was cut in half. The resentment wells up and focuses on the first child. She torments, "castrates," nags, screams, physically beats, and mentally tortures the child. The child eventually wanders in the half-world of schizophrenia.

At least that's the "socialization theory" of schizophrenia. However, there are ethnic variations in mental illness. Italians and Wasps differ in stress reactions and emotional responses, and the mentally ill do not suffer from the same kinds or rates of stress diseases as other people. What about male/female differences? We know that men have higher rates of coronary heart disease, ulcer, suicide, alcoholism, and lung cancer. Black women live longer than black men, and white women live nearly eight years longer than white men, nearly fourteen years longer than black men, and five years longer than black women.

Also, as women have moved into the world of work, and as it has become fashionable and socially acceptable for women to smoke and drink, we are slowly achieving equality in the area of disease. Heart-disease rates, lung-cancer rates, ulcer rates, and incidence of other diseases have all climbed year by year. While chemical substances contribute to soaring female death rates, stress takes its toll on the American woman. Even though female death rates climb, women generally have lower death rates than men. So do all female animals in relation to the males of the species.

Now, once again, we are looking at genetic factors. Cows live longer than bulls. Mares live longer than stallions. Since bulls and stallions do not suffer from pressure of taking subways and meeting clients' deadlines, we have to assume that there are genetic differences between males and females of most species. Females are built for bearing young and are less susceptible to disease. Female people last longer than male people for that specific reason.

Of course, the whole endocrine balance and hormonal system of the female is different from that of the male. For a women's-rights advocate like myself, that is nearly a heretical statement. Freud said, "Biology is destiny," and women were stuck for years with psychotherapeutic nonsense about our needing to reproduce and fulfill our biological destiny as mothers. That's not the kind of "difference" that I'm talking about, but, rather how men and women differ physically, psychologically, and socially in their reactions to stress.

Stress reactions may be highly related to levels of testosterone in the male and estrogen or progesterone in the female. In recent years a great deal of research has emerged on the problem of aggression. For example, males with low levels of testosterone exhibit low levels of aggressive behavior. However, the area of aggression and male/female differences is a rat's nest of undisciplined and very confusing research. Much of it has been directed by men who score aggression by little boys differently from aggression by little girls. Aggression, however, *is* learned behavior, not necessarily triggered by a special male hormone. Little girls are taught to be clean and tidy and not fight. Mothers tolerate dirty little boys and fathers encourage their sons to "beat the crap out of any bully who starts a fight with you." Thus a tomboy is a physically aggressive little girl who plays boys' games, beats up on her boy playmate, and generally doesn't act like a nice little girl. She is a "tomboy" not because of any superabundance of testosterone but probably because she had few girls as playmates, and parents who encouraged her "male" interests.

The tomboy probably will grow up to be a lawyer or doctor, not because of testosterone or being a tomboy but because of those same parents, who will encourage her to fulfill her ambitions in a male occupation. Yet her parents may not have done her a favor. Women who work continuously in their job die at about the same rate as men in the same occupation. The key word here is "continuously."

Women who work full time probably are subject to the same stresses and strains as men. Single women and single parents are subject to much greater strains than married men. Women workers have to get up in the morning, fight traffic, climb on subways, worry about deadlines, fuss over promotions, and, unfortunately, go home and take out their problems on their families. Working women are subject to the same illnesses as working men: heart attacks, high blood pressure, ulcers, and mounting rates of alcoholism. Just as we know that men in middle-management positions are subject to great stress and correspondingly high levels of stress-related illness, so also we expect that women will suffer the same kinds of trauma. Women in middle management are probably gulping Alka Seltzer and swilling Kaopectate as much as middle-management men do.

Maybe even more. Some psychological research on the "lone woman" shows that the woman alone in an organization or work group is often subject to more psychological pressure. Of course! It didn't really require more than a little common sense to figure out that the "outsider," the one who is somehow "different," is under pressure and scrutiny all the time. The first Jew in the country club, the first black general in the Air Force, the first woman on the New York Stock Exchange, or the first whoever will probably have clammy palms and a dry mouth for a long time. A society that gives lip service to the concept of *individuality* seems to punish those who are different.

And many working women have a double burden. Married, divorced, or widowed, the woman has to clean the house, make sure the kids are off to school, make dinner, do the laundry, see that the kids do their homework, pay for scout camp, bake cookies for the PTA, and somehow manage to do the work at the office. It is almost an unbearable burden for most women. No wonder, then, that more women than men swallow tranquilizers and barbiturates. Is it any surprise that women are seeking therapy, est, Yoga, and any other biofeedback tricks to solve these problems?

I don't mean to minimize the pain and suffering of men in our society but only point out that many women may be under more stress. Contrary to prevalent myths, most women work because they *have* to and not because they *want* to. The "have to" may be because a man has walked out and left a woman with three children, or the family "has to" have a house in the suburbs where the schools are better and the air is cleaner, or a disturbed child "has to" have in-depth therapy, or there is a need for a new color television set or new shoes or whatever. Everyone's standard of living, standard of life and needs, mounts higher and higher as income increases.

Whatever the reasons, women are under unwholesome strain. Are these stresses and strains any different from those of other generations? Who knows? A historical perspective may be interesting, but it is difficult to ascertain. Women who left the ghettoes of Russia or the drought-starved farms of Ireland and jumped on board ship to come to America may have endured far more than any of us are able to contemplate. My red-headed, freckle-faced Irish grandmother was one of these.

Granny's mother and father died in a flu epidemic and she was raised by her grandmother. Granny never said much about her grandmother except to tell me one time that my great-great-grandmother was a "sort of a witch." When she saw that I was having apoplexy of delight over a witch great-great-grandmother, she hastened to explain, "Well, she really wasn't a witch but only sort of cured people." Be that as it may, the great-great-grandmother died, the Black and Tans were all over Ireland, the Micks and the Orangeman were beating each other up regularly, and martial law was imminent. So Granny decided that she had had enough of this nonsense and she waltzed down to the boat quay and plunked some money on the counter.

"How far will that take me?" she asked the ticket salesman.

"Probably as far as Scotland and no more," he replied.

"Done!" said Granny, and she picked up her little bag and jumped on the boat.

And that is how Mary Feeney arrived in Scotland, met a Highland Scot engineer, married him, and then harassed him until he emigrated to Canada. Her life was never still and hardly free from strain or stress. After World War I my grandfather returned gassed, filled with shrapnel, and unable to work fully again. Granny held the family together, worked, put two girls through school, cared for her ailing husband, and saw her way through the Depression, World War II, and the death of her beloved David. She never lost her sense of humor or her independence. At eighty-four, she came crashing into my parents' house one night mad as a wet hen. She had just come from her first meeting of the Golden Age Club and was absolutely furious.

"They want to sit around and play cards and talk about

the good old days," she fumed. "I want to dance and drink a little whiskey. They're old fuddie duddies and I hate them," she moaned in her lilting Irish brogue. And she danced and she had her wee nip of whiskey and cracked jokes every day of her life. When she was still in her eighties she came to me and confessed that she was worried about the few strands of white that had crept into her carrot-red hair.

"I know that all you young girls do something with your hair and I think that you ought to help your poor old Granny out," she cajoled me.

When I tried to explain as delicately as possible that no cosmetic company in the world bottled her brand of yellow-red-carrot-fire hair, she threw a fit and flounced out of the house, vowing never to speak to such an upstart again. When I saw her a few days later, she smirked at me and announced that she had figured everything out. Using some sort of peroxide-henna mix, courtesy of her local pharmacist, she succeeded in dyeing her recalcitrant white strands back to their original and thoroughly awful color.

Not only was my Granny a character but, unbeknownst to me at that time, she was a super role model for a young, impressionable little girl. My Granny was indomitable; she had spirit, spunk, fire, and gumption enough for a passel of legionnaires. She cooked and sewed, cleaned, yelled at her daughters, picked the shrapnel out of her husband's wounds, sat by his bedside at the hospital, and taught her granddaughter what courage was all about. Whenever the proverbial wolf arrived at Granny's door, she opened the door, kicked him in the chin, hit him over the head with a broom, and sent him on his way. She was a survivor. She had little religious faith to sustain her and would have hooted over Esalen, Yoga, est, and psychotherapy. Granny didn't die peacefully. She railed at her illness and cursed at her doctors. She didn't nibble at life but ate it in great big gulps. Granny was a fierce woman who thrived on stress and adversity.

There are few of that breed around. The sons and daughters of immigrants who arrived here in steerage seek out magic panaceas by pills, booze, psychiatrists, new religions, and how-to books. Granny epitomized what David Riesman calls the "inner-directed personality." She didn't wonder whether or not she was right. She *knew* it. Introspection was a luxury that Granny—and most of her generation—couldn't afford.

Granny would never have spent endless hours wondering about anal-oral fixations, toilet-training traumas, open marriages, or the existential meaning of life. Life, for Granny, was to be lived and enjoyed. Hers was not a vale of tears but a bubbling, burbling adventure to be alternately sworn at or sweet-talked. So, in those hours when deadlines and hostile enemies close in on me, at three o'clock in the morning, I remember a slim-hipped, freckle-faced young girl facing down the ticket master on the dockside and think that those genes are my heritage—and then go to bed.

But not all of us have a pixie-leprechaun grandmother to see us through the evil hours of the morning. Most of us have been traumatized by Freud and how-to book writers. We seek inner meaning in every ordinary action and psychologize ourselves to death. Some of us cannot survive very well and turn to a whole host of coping mechanisms not only to get us through the night but the next day and then, again, the next night.

An ordinary dose of common sense seems to be missing in this daily and nightly struggle. We love to listen to the afternoon talk-show philosophers and seek the perpetual Holy Grail of self-enlightenment. We are indeed the "me" generation. NOW is the magic word. Freedom NOW. Sexual fulfillment NOW. Instant mashed potatoes and instant nirvana—NOW. David Riesman's outer-directed man is like a weather vane blowing in the wind, desperately trying to catch other people's moods. He plans his actions in tune with their approbation. His vocabulary is peppered with words like "on the other hand," "but," and "let's look at both sides." He is sophisticated, cultured, tolerant, and all too often willing to sell his soul in order not to be thought rigid or stuffy.

The outer-directed man or woman is constantly barraged and assailed by the mass media, who give him or her new ways of behaving and thinking. NBC News, *Penthouse*, *Oui*, *Playgirl*, *Playboy*, Heff's cute philosophy, and the pseudoscience of *Psychology Today* combined with advice columns from *Ladies' Home Journal*, *Redbook*, and *McCall's* all tell the outer-directed person to look inward, seek personal pleasure to the exclusion of family, home, and national ethos. Meditate for a moment on the image of a forty-fiftyish man who swizzles Pepsi Cola incessantly, cannot work in an office, is unable to maintain enduring friendships, must constantly be surrounded by a non-stop house party, and chooses a rabbit fertility symbol for his corporate logo: *he is the* arbiter of swinging American culture. Is it any surprise, then, that we are confused?

A rabbit is a strange cultural symbol. What a weird transformation of values from Stars and Bars to a Bunny. We are a nation of wanderers and cultists. Stress and strain. Skin rashes, low back pain, migraines, cystitis, diverticulitis, overweight, and underweight are harbingers of the *Weltschmerz* we all feel. *Weltschmerz* means "world pain." Perhaps that's what our stresses and strains and psychosomatic illnesses are all about: world pain. Our world sadness may be the result of a wrenching divorce, worry over nuclear holocaust, teen-age rebellion, TV documentaries on mass starvation, or a child who has just failed grade two. We do suffer from world pain. Perhaps no more and no less than the Greeks or the crusaders, but many of us have a sense of normlessness, *Angst*, nothingness, or what sociologists call *anomie*. We are a generation torn from our foundations. One in every five families in the United States move every year. Traditional churches like the Roman Catholic and Episcopalian change their age-old liturgical rites and ceremonies. There is no mother next door to help you with the baby's rash. Scandals rock Congress. The dollar falls on the international money markets. We search about earnestly looking for firm answers to new problems. Those who went through teen-age drinking bouts in the 1950s cannot comprehend drug traffic in the high schools of the 1970s. We buy how-to books and eagerly tune in to the television talk-show gurus for the latest version of mass-media truth.

David Riesman wrote about "inner-directed" and "outer-directed" persons. Most of us are inner-directed, or high need-achieving, nice, middle-class people who were raised by nice, middle-class people in a reasonably secure, black-and-white world. Our parents and we ourselves simply knew the right thing to do. The right thing ranges from wearing white gloves to Sunday school to fighting Hitler. That's the way things are. The outer-directed person is the classic man in the gray flannel suit who toadies up to his boss, who puts the corporate ethos ahead of family, who is a weather vane anticipating others' reactions, and who has problems deciding who he *really* is. The outer-directed man sounds awfully familiar: he is the haunted, confused hero of so many trashy modern novels. And so we worry on and on. Worry over mortgages, success, failure, children, marriage. We pay terrible prices for our worries.

Like the dog chasing its tail, mental stress produces physical and psychological reactions which trigger more stress. The woman who worries and frets about her husband's infidelity gets a serious skin rash; she can't sleep because of the itching rash and she now worries over the mounting doctor bills. She and her husband can't have sex because her skin is so tender. Her husband continues and even increases his sordid little affairs. And the pattern continues on and on.

While psychologists and psychiatrists write about "coping mechanisms," most of us think in terms of consciously revamping our life style. One method of coping, for example, is to get rid of the problem: divorce your husband or quit your job. Another is to go into depth therapy and try to understand your particular psychological hang-ups. Primal scream therapy is one way that psychiatrists are trying to loosen people up. In primal scream therapy, the patient yells and screams and pounds the floor and releases previously bottled-up hostility and tension. Sometimes it works and sometimes it doesn't. I always wonder what happens when you scream your heart out to the tune of fifty dollars an hour. Does that mean that you now can go home and scream imprecations at the kids and your husband? Does it mean that you will feel emotionally released and your inhibitions will be forever unleashed? Frankly, I hope not.

Primal scream and general psychotherapy aside, illness is a coping mechanism. After all, you can't "help" getting sick. Can you? A person who is sick requires tender loving care, attention, chicken soup, sympathy, and lots and lots of ego strokes. Illness effectively solves a lot of problems. If a man hates his job, he has a heart attack and his doctor tells him to quit his job. A woman who hates her children and hates housework develops a bad back. She cannot lift anything, has problems hobbling around the house, and is in continual pain. She is in and out of hospitals for spinal fusions, disk operations, and physical therapy. In the meantime, the family has to rally around and perform her household tasks. Voilà! The problem of how to get out of housework is solved.

The beauty of psychosomatic illness is that it provides a ready excuse for *not* doing what you didn't want to do anyway. Also, illness helps to make the parties who contributed to the illness feel guilty. It's a grown-up version of the bed-wetting game.

A child who wakes up in the middle of the night with a soiled bed wails, "I didn't mean to do it." The tight-lipped parent cleans up the bed, changes the sheets, puts dry pajamas on the five-year-old, or ten-year-old, or thirteen-year-old. The next night and the next night for years, the pattern repeats itself. Conferences with pediatricians, psychiatrists, teachers, and other parents don't seem to help at all. How can the parent get angry at the child who soils himself while asleep? After all, he couldn't help it. Could he? What most parents don't understand about bed wetting is that it is a hostile reaction on the part of the child.

The bed wetter is very very angry at his parents for some reason. Perhaps the parents toilet-trained him too harshly. Maybe the parents pay too much attention to a brother or sister. Perhaps these parents demand too much from an ordinary little boy or girl. The kid well understands that the parents get upset about a kid who soils his or her bed. The child wets the bed. The parents get angry. The child wails that he (or she) couldn't help it. The parents feel guilty about being angry at a little child who loses control over his (or her) bladder in the middle of the night. And the cycle continues for years.

It's the same thing with psychosomatic illness. Husbands feel guilty that their wives have bad backs, and bosses are filled with remorse over an employee's heart attack. It's like an angry little child stamping his (or her) foot and saying, "I'll make you sorry that you were mean to me." On the other hand, there are lots of husbands and bosses who really don't give a damn about spouse or employee. They not only refuse to feel guilt, some of them even enjoy the havoc that they wreak on other people. One of my bosses leaned across his desk and bellowed at me, "Just remember this! I *give* ulcers, I don't *get* them."

He certainly did. His office staff lived in daily fear of his outbursts and trembled at night when the telephone rang. Since we were paid well, he assumed that he had life-and-death and twenty-four-hour-a-day control over us. Most of us were caught in a tight job-market situation and our job mobility was limited. He knew it. He abused us. Whenever he was absent from the office, several of the senior staff members would gather for coffee and meditate on why we willingly suffered his abuse. While we all agreed that we were basically masochistic, the true answer came to money. Occasionally someone would decide that the good life in Santa Fe outweighed Washington pressure, but most of us perversely hung on to our wretched but highly paid positions.

We all reacted adversely to our wretched jobs: Three divorces. One stroke. One heart attack. Young male staffers reported impotency. Several secretaries said that they couldn't seem to get pregnant. Many of us sought other jobs. But the boss still yells and carries on. The organization survives. The psychic pain continues.

Now, both the men and the women in that office were subject to the same strains. Yet the men seemed to suffer more adverse reactions than did the women. Over a period of years, I tried to figure out what the salient differences between the men and the women were. One thing that was most evident was that more women were in low-level positions and *didn't* catch the same kind of flack as the middle-management males. But the few middle-management females were equally as harassed. The only one who seemed to work with any sense of equanimity was Holly, who kept reminding us that she was exactly eighteen months to retirement and holding. She was the only one—man or woman—who had any sense that her travail would soon be over.

With the major exception of Holly, we all began to pay

a terrible price for our paychecks. The women were paying some prices in women's physiology. Irregular menstruation. Menstrual problems. Cramping. Inability to get pregnant. Miscarriages. Over coffee, we told each other our physical and personal problems. No matter if a woman was a high-level researcher or a secretary, each seemed to be suffering from acute physiological stress related to menstruation or pregnancy. There was a decided difference in the actual stress response *within* the office, however.

When a researcher caught a dressing down, she would slam doors and sulk in her office. A secretary would usually burst into tears and storm out of the office and hide in the ladies' washroom. I did everything: slammed doors, sulked, cried, hid in the women's washroom, and swore a lot. All the women were allowed much more leeway in expressing emotion and probably were better off than the cardiac-prone male researchers.

One office does not make a full-blown theory, but it started me on the track of trying to discern the differences between male and female stress reactions. Since male plumbing and female plumbing are different, I decided to investigate research on menstruation, pregnancy, menopause, and frigidity. What could physiologists, psychologists, and biologists tell me about male-female differences in relation to cancer, drug addiction, and alcoholism? To my surprise I found that there are more data on differences between male and female rats than there are on differences between male and female humans.

Frankly, I wonder now at my surprise. There are male medicine and male research. Since more men are biochemists and physiologists and medical doctors, obviously men will study their favorite subject—men—rather than take a look at human females. Even in most of the research dealing with women, researchers present their findings under the thinly disguised rubric of "how silly women really are."

Realizing that many of the findings are suspect and extrapolating from rats and rabbits, let us look at differences between men and women on stress reactions. Based on case studies and interviews, we will see the coping mechanisms —good and bad—that women use to survive. The coping methods range from successfully fighting cancer, to succumbing to a heart attack, to years of psychiatric therapy, to abuse of alcohol or pills.

2

The Unique Case:
West Point

T O be the first in anything is stressful: the first runner in a race, the first black to enter a southern university, the first speaker in a debating conference, the first woman to graduate from a male Ivy League college, or the first woman firefighter in Los Angeles. Personal anecdotes, diaries, interviews, and television talk shows gives us *some* idea of what the stress and personal toll of being the first means for a person. But only in recent years have sociologists—primarily *women* sociologists—investigated what being a woman in a man's world really means.

Women can fulfill a multitude of roles. A growth toward personal happiness is the goal of all people, male and fe-

male. No one role is more "appropriate" to women than
another. Being a mother is not the ultimate role for a
woman. Nor is a celibate nun a goal to be condoned or
condemned. Sexual egalitarianism, women's liberation,
feminism, and self-fulfillment can all complement each
other.

Some people feel that women ought not to become doctors, lawyers, pilots, or even President or Vice-President of
the United States. Current ferment within Congress, arguments raging in the letters-to-the-editor columns of newspapers across the United States, ERA foes hurling epithets
and invective at each other—all show the depth of anger
and hurt in this nation over role reversal and changing sex-
role attitudes. Controversy surrounding the admission of
women to the military academies is one example. Let us,
then, examine what happened to the first class of women
cadets at West Point.

Project Athena

Athena is the Greek goddess of war, the guardian of the
U. S. Women's Army Corps, and also the patron of the
U. S. Military Academy (West Point). The Department of
Behavioral Sciences at West Point named its study on the
integration of women at West Point "Project Athena" and
I was appointed codirector. Our first year was critical, because it was during that year that the women cadets were
the *only* women cadets. The more women in an institution
(whether Princeton, Harvard, or West Point) the easier
the situation becomes. Once their very uniqueness has
worn off, women cease to be the butt of jokes, hostility,

favoritism, or public scrutiny. So the following pages report only the first year of women in a unique situation—a situation unknown to any woman in the history of the world. For no woman has ever before attended a male military academy.

A word of caution. The tale has yet to be told up to 1980, when the first women will graduate. Since West Pointers are obligated to serve five years after graduation, 1985 is also an important year, to determine how many women (and men) of the class of 1980 will opt for a lifetime career within the U. S. Army. The years 2000, 2005, and 2010 are crucial. In these years, most graduates (male and female) of the class of 1980 who chose the Army as a career will know which of the confreres have reached the rank of at least brigadier general. So, much more research is needed to complete the picture.

Background

Admitting women to military academies formed the base for debate that raged for years within and without Congress and the Department of Defense, and in the press. The Army, the Department of Defense, and West Point opposed the admission of women to the military academy. This opposition was predicated on the assertion that service academies exist to develop combat leaders. Since national policy excludes women from serving in combat units, there was no place for women at the academies. A former superintendent, Lieutenant General William Knowlton, addressed the Military Personnel Subcommittee in April of 1974, stating:

I therefore believe that admission of women to the Academy would seriously detract from the Academy's mission and, hence, from the ability of the United States Army to insure the peace.

Because of the finite physical facilities at the Academy, any admission of women would necessarily reduce the number of male graduates. So long as women were not permitted to serve in combat roles or in combat units, the effect would be to decrease the number of exceptionally qualified, Regular Army career combat officers. *The existence of other sources of commissioned officers does not militate for a contrary conclusion since the purpose for the establishment of the Academy was to provide the nucleus for the Regular Army's combat officers.* The Academy has in fact provided this nucleus, and its graduates continue to provide the ethos of the Army.

If, notwithstanding the disqualification of women *for combat, they were nevertheless required to meet the demands of the Academy's present, combat-oriented curriculum, I would anticipate several adverse consequences.* First, although some women could no doubt meet the physical rigors demanded, I would expect the dropout rate among females to be substantially higher than for males. Indeed, even as to those women who could meet the physical demands, the very fact of being required to engage in unpleasant physical activities *in order to prepare for a combat role* which they will never fill could well act to increase this dropout rate. Needless to say, any increase in the dropout rate among the Corps of Cadets, in addition to adversely affecting morale, could well seriously impede the Academy's mission. Second, it could well cause women who would otherwise choose an Army career to leave the Army for civilian pursuits, with obvious detrimental effects on this branch of service. Third, and not to be discounted, certain of the training can endanger the well-being of women cadets.

In the alternative, if the Academy were required by the Court to adopt a new educational philosophy and provide a different kind of program leading to commissioning for women, the Army and the nation would, in my professional judgment, be ill-served. It would be difficult to assign only women to these programs on the basis of their sex for legal, if not for policy, reasons; and many men not now admitted to the Academy because of disqualification for combat would have a legitimate claim for admittance. This would lessen the number of *males being trained for careers as combat officers* and would inevitably reduce the unity, morale, and efficiency of the Corps of Cadets.

Those who felt that women should be admitted to the academies were equally as firm in their assertions. Congressman Dante B. Fascell, of Florida, told the Military Personnel Subcommittee in June of 1974:

At issue is whether we want the best qualified person admitted to our service academies, or whether we want the best qualified male. I say, we need the best qualified person.

H.R. 11276 would eliminate the exemption from the prohibition of sex discrimination provisions of the Education Amendments of 1972 which now exists for the service academies. Further, it would bring those sections of the U. S. Code relating to admission requirements at each of the academies in conformance with the non-discrimination policy.

The Congress has repeatedly affirmed that discrimination of any kind, including sex discrimination, is clearly wrong and a violation of basic Constitutional guarantees. The Congress and the federal government must continue the leadership role in breaking down the traditional sex barriers which still deny equal opportunities to women.

The purpose of the service academies is to train highly skilled and motivated officers for the armed forces who will rise to top leadership positions in the services. There is no reason that young women should not be given the opportunity to have this education benefit and to then serve as officers in the armed forces. The myth of the weaker sex has long been disproven, and I feel certain that there are many women in this country who could easily withstand the tough physical training undergone by our Army, Navy and Air Force cadets.

Until recently, women have had to pay for their own education and preparation for the armed services. Some progress has been made. The Reserve Officer Training Corps scholarship program has recently been opened to women.

But this is not equality. Women should have the same opportunities as men for the outstanding training available at the service academies. And that means eliminating the current admission restrictions and opening up the academies to qualified women applicants.

The Department of Defense argues that the mission of the service academies is to train officers to fill combat positions, and that women are unsuited for such positions. This argument assumes, first, a need only for combat leadership which assumes a constant and perpetual state of combat—assumptions I find inherently chilling. It also assumes that women are, somehow, not qualified for such responsibilities. The veracity of that assumption is being tested daily.

Women are increasingly proving that they are fully qualified to assume responsibilities formerly considered appropriate only for men. For example, police forces throughout the country are hiring a growing number of women. And those women are not restricted to desk jobs or "meter-maid" roles. They are trained in self-defense and criminal apprehension techniques and assigned to patrol duty just as their male counterparts.

Mr. Chairman, the nation's armed forces need the best possible personnel and leadership. Current admission policy effectively excludes half of the nation's potential officers. Not only is such a policy inequitable and discriminatory, but it is not in the best interest of our defense preparedness.

Our service academies provide an excellent—indeed the best—training ground for the future officers on whom our armed forces personnel and policy depend. We must make sure that the most capable and best qualified persons receive that training. And to make sure that happens, we must allow women applicants to compete for academy appointments.

In May of 1975, the House of Representatives voted 303 to 96 to admit women to the national service academies. In June of 1975, the Senate voted to admit women. On October 7, 1975, President Gerald Ford signed the Defense Appropriation Authorization Act of 1976 (Public Law 94–106) with the "Stratton amendment" on admissions of women to the academies. The law states:

. . . The Secretaries of the Military Departments concerned shall take such action as may be necessary and appropriate to insure that (1) female individuals shall be eligible for appointment and admission to the service academy concerned, beginning with appointment to such academy for the class beginning in calendar year 1976, and (2) the academic and other relevant standards required for appointment, (admissions) training, graduation, and commissioning of female individuals shall be the same as those required for male individuals, except for those minimum essential adjustments in such standards required because of physiological differences between male and female individuals.

In a letter to academy alumni in the December 1975 West Point alumni magazine, *Assembly*, the superintendent, Lieutenant General Sidney B. Berry, wrote:

Women are coming to West Point. Since the House and the Senate approved the legislation last spring, we at West Point have worked positively, professionally and effectively to prepare for the admission of women. We have our orders, and it is our responsibility to implement them to the best of our ability. Since June, I personally have devoted more time, thought, energy and effort to preparing West Point for the admission of women than to any other single matter. Our planning is now complete and has been approved by the Chief of Staff and Secretary of the Army. I am confident that our planning is sound.

The mission of the Military Academy remains intact: to educate and train top quality solider-leaders for the United States Army. The Corps of Cadets will continue to be the unified, talented group of aspirant Army officers who have distinguished the Long Gray Line for more than 173 years. Since it is the will of Congress and the President, we are welcoming women candidates as we welcome men candidates to West Point. We expect to make this change smoothly and efficiently.

The law does provide for certain adjustments in some training because of physiological differences between men and women. Our basic philosophy is this: all cadets should undergo common training and education; there will be minimum necessary adjustments made for women cadets; where adjustments are appropriate, women cadets will undergo training equivalent to that of men cadets.

Our business at West Point is to serve the needs of the Regular Army officer corps. There are women in that corps. If the officer preparation at the Military Academy is important for the excellence of the Army, then women officers can benefit by West Point's education and training. The process of admitting women potentially expands the pool of qualified candidates—men and women—from which we select our outstanding cadets every year. This could raise the academic standards at West Point. Men and women cadets will learn to work together professionally and objectively—a good preparation for life in the Army and, generally, in American society.

Planning and Preparing

West Point then began long and detailed preparation for the incoming women cadets. Hart, Schaffner & Marx designed new women's uniforms. West Point redesigned bathrooms for women. High-ranking military and civilian personnel visited West Point and consulted with faculty and staff regarding women's psychological, sociological, and physical needs. The military academy and staff sought advice and counsel from many sources. Women were coming and had to be integrated into the corps with as little fuss as possible. Basic to all planning was West Point's decision to integrate women in the barracks area. Thus, women shared rooms with women cadets on the same floor as men in their cadet companies, rather than all women from different companies being isolated in one wing or on a separate floor. The billeting decision was reinforced by the wording of the Stratton amendment, which said that adjustment would be made only because of "physiological differences between male and female individuals."

However, when West Point faculty, particularly the staff of the Department of Physical Education, examined physiological research on adolescents, they found that little hard data existed comparing males and females. In addition, little research compared men and women in physical fitness, and what comparisons existed were often outdated in light of increased physical fitness and new programs for girls in the high schools. West Point's Department of Education then designed and monitored several long-ranging projects comparing male and female prowess.

The Department of Physical Education continued its research, while other staff and faculty visited Princeton, Yale, the Merchant Marine Academy (which had first admitted women in September 1975), and the U. S. Women's Army Corps centers at Forts McClellan and Jackson. The Department of Behavioral Science and Leadership surveyed cadets and faculty on several scales concerning attitudes toward women. Interestingly enough, the predominantly male faculty were more "liberal" toward women than the all-male student cadets. However, this result is not surprising, since the faculty and staff have higher levels of education and have worked with women enlisted and women officers. Also, the students' attitudes were the result of several years of the academy "stonewalling" against the admission of women.

While all these plans were underway, the initial task was to find women candidates. West Point mailed letters to 18,643 high school counselors informing them of the new law. The West Point Admissions Office sent a letter to approximately two thousand women who had applied for Reserve Officer Training Corps (ROTC) scholarships in 1974 and 1975, to inform them that West Point was now open to women. A computer search by the American College Testing Program found twenty-two hundred women with an interest in science, mathematics, and the military. Finally, 867 files were opened, 631 women were nominated and examined, and 148 were offered admission. Since twenty-eight women declined and one was medically disqualified, the academy finally admitted 119 women. Who were these women?

What Kind of Girl Goes to West Point?

Time and time again, people would ask me in a somewhat deprecating tone, "What kind of girl goes to West Point?" The answer is, of course, the same kind of girl who would go to an engineering school or the same kind of personality and background as the men who enter West Point. Entrance to West Point is a complicated procedure, but basically candidates are chosen on the basis of three areas: high school grades, leadership ability, and physical fitness. West Point's Department of Physical Education devised different standards of physical fitness for women, based on their research showing that women would systematically fail a *male* test, involving chin-ups or push-ups. The major modification was a "flexed-arm hang," in which women hang from a bar in the same position as for a chin-up and are timed for the number of seconds they can hold this position.

Without belaboring the differences in physical fitness and body strength, the women were shorter and lighter than the men. Intellectually, however, the women had somewhat higher SAT (Scholastic Aptitude Test) scores than the men cadets of the class of 1980. Ninety per cent of the women surpassed the male thirty-third percentile, while (by definition) only 66 per cent of the men were in this category. Like most high school graduate women, the female plebes were higher in verbal skills and English proficiency than the men and slightly lower than the men in mathematical skills. Many more women (31 per cent) had had one or two years of college, in comparison with the incoming male cadets—only 14 per cent of whom were transfers from other colleges. Of course, this makes perfect sense for the class of 1980, because women who might have wanted to attend West Point prior to 1975 were unable to do so because of legal prohibitions. From now on, each year will see fewer women with some college. (The academy does not give credit for previous college experience.)

Women cadets came to West Point for the same reasons as the men: to receive a high-quality education and to train to become officers in the United States Army. Both male and female cadets of the class of 1980 were highly ambitious and had a firm and confident outlook on life. Why not? These young men and women had visible proof, through their high school grades, their scouting and community activities, their nominations to the National Honor Society, and their awards in sports activities, that they were indeed some of the finest young people in the United States. When I read the biographies of these young people (both male and female), I was constantly struck by their intensely high caliber. Today, it is quite fashionable to moan over the decadent youth of the United States. But these young men and women belie any and all prophets of doom. Yet, West Point itself was in the throes of agony—for reasons utterly unconnected with the issue of women.

The Cheating Scandal

Up to this point, it might seem that the admission of women at West Point was a *fait accompli*, existing in a vacuum. This was not so. While feverish activity surrounded the admission of women to West Point, the academy itself was undergoing public scrutiny, criticism, lawsuits, counter lawsuits, resignations, Congressional investigation, and unmitigating media coverage.

In March 1976, the Electrical Engineering Department gave second classmen (juniors) a take-home examination. In April, the department forwarded to the Cadet Honor Committee the names of cadets believed to have collaborated on the assignment. Cadet honor boards met, civilian and military lawyers prosecuted and defended, and 152 cadets were dismissed. Arguments raged in the Congress and within and without the Department of the Army and the Department of Defense. The Secretary of the Army announced a plan whereby a cadet who had cheated on the exam or who had resigned in connection with the incident would be eligible for readmission after one year. The Borman Commission conducted an in-depth analysis of the situation at West Point and concluded that some reforms and reorganization were necessary to preserve the vital concept of West Point and the important West Point Honor Code.

So the reader must realize that the plebes who entered West Point on July 6, 1977, entered an atmosphere fraught with tension—more from the cheating scandal than from the fact that this class contained women cadets.

The First Summer

During July and August of 1976, men and women cadets went through all phases of Cadet Basic Training together. From the agonizing moment of saying good-by to family and friends, to the trauma of the first haircut, through marches, weapons training, and camping and hiking, the women kept up with the men. Even though women tired more easily and experienced more injuries related to fatigue, by the end of the summer the cadet upperclassmen and members of the West Point faculty and staff had just reason to be proud of their women.

While 16 per cent of the women as compared to 10 per cent of the men resigned by the end of the first summer, there were no differences between women and men in reasons for leaving West Point. Both men and women who resigned tended to state that they dislike military discipline and regimentation. Few women stated that they felt that there was inherent sex bias or discrimination.

Since West Point's Project Athena had surveyed male

cadets in the spring of 1976 and found that there was a decided prejudice against women in general and women cadets in particular, academy officials had inundated cadets with a program of lectures, workshops, and human-relations seminars. Brigadier General Walter Ulmer specifically stated that no upperclassmen were to denigrate women cadets in any way. Also, four women U. S. Army officers were assigned to the academy. These women officers served as role models for the women cadets, counselors to the women cadets, and more importantly, examples to the male cadets of professional competence and excellence. These programs eased the women cadets' acceptance.

The School Year

Things were not completely rosy and there were isolated instances of jokes in bad taste and teasing on the part of the male cadets. However, the West Point women were (and are) success-oriented people who have a higher self-concept than women in other four-year colleges. For example, 95 per cent of the West Point women, compared to 57 per cent of women college students in other four-year colleges, felt that they had superior academic ability; 86 per cent of the West Point women, compared to 43 per cent of other women college students, stated that they had high leadership ability, and not too surprisingly at all, 94 per cent of the West Point women, compared to 66 per cent of the other women, feel that they have a strong drive to achieve. These women knew their own strengths and weaknesses. However, the West Point *men* also score higher on these items than men in the sample of other four-year colleges. Nonetheless, for men the magnitude of difference was not as great.

The women were relatively unflappable. But they still suffered from the strain of being unique. Probably the most frustrating aspect of the first year was the unceasing media coverage of women cadets. From the first day, in July, throughout the whole year, ABC, NBC, CBS, *McCall's* magazine, the New York *Times*, the Detroit *News*, and newspaper reporters from throughout the United States—whatever the home town of whichever woman plebe—were all there. Women cadets were featured in magazines and newspapers throughout the world.

No wonder, then, that the male cadets resented the undue publicity given to women cadets. Many women agreed that their resentment was justified. The women were tired of being media freaks and wanted to be let alone. They resented being interviewed, poked, prodded, tested, and examined by reporters, women officers, and West Point counselors. They were tired of all the attention. These women had come to West Point to receive an education and train for a career as an officer, not to be in the pages of newspapers and magazines.

Also, male cadets began to ridicule women's higher-pitched voices as not a "command voice," and men said that the women's shorter marching strides were not "military." Some women began to worry that they were adopting masculine standards of behavior. Some worried over the conflict between "femininity" and the "masculine" world of West Point. The long hours of study, their personal conflicts, the sometimes good-natured and sometimes barbed teasing, took a toll. Nearly 56 per cent of the West

Point women reported that they had menstrual problems. Now, was this a feature of being a woman at West Point? Or do males suffer equal stress and we are unable to measure it? At this juncture, we don't know. I suspect that the first year at any college, and at West Point in particular, is stressful for any young man or woman. Separation from family support, pressure to maintain high grades, and general adolescent role confusion add up to stress—whether at the military academy or at Podunk U. But the first year at West Point is designed specifically to test the mettle of the plebe. Whether or not the reader agrees with this philosophy is unimportant. West Point cadets live under a monastic and strict set of rules. Uniform regulations, a strict honor code, rules: for marching, lights out, shining shoes. Life at the military academy is regimented and highly regulated. It is, therefore, stressful.

Both men and women are under extreme stress during their first year at West Point. However, by the end of May 1978, 34.5 per cent, or forty-one, of the original 119 women had resigned, and 31.6 per cent, or 431, of the original 1,366 men had resigned. Thus, in terms of actual percentage of attrition, men and women were nearly equal.

Things Get Better

Rather than focusing on the women who left, let us look at the women who stayed. As the year progressed, fewer and fewer reporters came to interview the women cadets. The women plebes soon moved into the mainstream of West Point life. Women joined the cheerleading squad, ski patrol, music and drama clubs, and even had their own discussion seminar. But the group that formed a catalyst for the integration of women at West Point was the Sugar Smacks: the West Point women's basketball team (which the male cadets first regarded as a joke).

But as the season continued, the women's basketball team became the pride of West Point. Since the West Point women marched, ran, and jogged every day, the physical condition of the basketball-team members was excellent. The West Point women outran, outplayed, overwhelmed, and overpowered their opponents. Given West Point's emphasis on fair play and team support, male cadets began to attend women's basketball games. Seesaw battles back and forth on the floor usually resulted in West Point wins. Cheers of "Go, girls!" soon changed to "USMA! USMA! USMA!" The girls were no longer girls but West Point cadets. With a record of fourteen wins and five losses, the Sugar Smacks helped bond women cadets to the corps.

The Sugar Smacks were not the only bonding force, but they were a focus of male approval. Men who wanted to support their sister cadets did so in the approved way of cheering teams in the sports arena. The Sugar Smacks were winners, and winning is part of West Point tradition. The other young women plebes of the class of 1980 were winners also. They had shown during the first summer that they could withstand heat, long marches, physical demands, and emotional stress. The women earned their chevrons in the classrooms but did not surpass the men. Fifty-five per cent of the West Point women stood in the top half of their class. In short, the West Point women acted much like the West Point men. Some were high in leadership ability and some were high in academic ability and some were outstanding sportswomen. Some were all three. Some weren't any. Day by day throughout the academic year, the women showed the men that women cadets were competent young people.

The West Point women's experience is scarcely begun, but it is a lodestar and a courageous example of what intelligent, self-confident, well-adjusted young women can do. This is coping at its best. West Point adjusted and prepared for an alien force: women. The women came to West Point and earned the grudging admiration of faculty, staff, and fellow students. The women came with trepidation but supreme self-assurance. They worried over their own self-image; they wanted to be accepted; they struggled to maintain their dignity in the face of unmerciful teasing. These young women survived the first year and are well on their way to obtain their second lieutenants' bars. I would gladly claim any one of them as my daughter. Lucky the nation and the armed service that can claim any one of them.

3

Women in Other Times and Current Cultures

Wᴴᴵʟᴇ women at military academies are in the fore-front of social change, they represent only a portion of the vital shifts occurring in the United States today. No one who has lived through the trauma of the 1960s and on into the somewhat reformist 1970s can be untouched by this reaffirmation of women's liberation. Even though "women's libber" is a pejorative term, still women are asking, begging, demanding, and often receiving what they feel is their just due. However, note that I used the word "reaffirmation" of women's rights. The 1920s and 1930s were closer to the 1970s than many people realize.

When Betty Friedan wrote *The Feminine Mystique*, she

pointed out that more doctorates and professional degrees, *in absolute numbers*, were granted to women in the 1930s than to women in the 1950s. Thus she developed the central thesis of her book, that there was a Madison Avenue ethos of a "feminine mystique" to get women out of the workplace and back to the home as consumers only. Friedan's book, which appeared in 1963, spoke to the terrible fears and unresolved longings of thousands upon thousands of women who had adopted the "feminine mystique" and were miserable in their suburban homes. Whether or not Friedan wants to accept the laurel or not, she is the founder and one of the great driving forces behind the women's movement of the 1960s. Betty Friedan's book *It Changed My Life*, which appeared in 1976, is a very personalized and very much ignored account of how the women's movement changed not only *her* life but that of many thousands of women.

It Changed Everyone's Life

With Friedan's analysis of the feminine mystique, and research on women by women social scientists, and writings by women journalists on women, a stirring began in the land. Women organized into small consciousness-raising groups. Women teachers objected to sex stereotyping in children's books. Mothers and teachers agreed that it was wrong to portray girls practicing to be mommies while boys were shown as future pilots and engineers. The same mothers and teachers began to demand an end to sex-role typing of toys. Lionel trains were for girls as well as boys. Chemistry and Erector sets were meant for both boys and girls. And there was a minor movement to allow boys to play with dolls, but "G.I. Joe" seemed to be the only result of that campaign.

Mothers who wanted their girls to learn mathematics were themselves slowly returning to the labor force. As divorce rates climbed, more women *had* to work and found that they were not given equal pay for equal work. While critics of the women's movement said that the women's libbers were primarily white middle-class women—and they were right—blue-collar women fought for the right to be telephone linemen and firefighters and coal miners and construction workers. We changed words from "chairman" to "chairperson," but fisherperson and cowperson never entered the common vocabulary. *Ms.* is not only a magazine but a designation for a woman that doesn't tell anyone whether or not she is a single, divorced, or married woman, as do "Miss" and "Mrs.". Talk shows delighted in pitting Gloria Steinem against Phyllis Shlafly. Phil Donahue, Merv Griffin, and other purveyors of American culture jumped on the women's bandwagon.

Amid snickers and sneers, social change occured. Billie Jean King and Bobby Riggs slugged it out for a lot of money and a lot of Madison Avenue hype, but the results were spectacular. Billie Jean King, Margaret Court, Evonne Goolagong, and Olga Korbut became new role models for young American women. Today, as the result of the new sports stars and some vicious court battles over equal facilities and equal rights, girls are playing on the same teams as boys or at least are playing what used to be exclusively boys' sports. My own, home-grown soccer star, Patrick, age seven, rates his co-ed team in a new, non-sexist way. Patrick tells me that "Jimmie-Joe is the best player on the team, Maureen is next, and I'm the third best." Patrick and Maureen are portents of the new wave in the new future.

For, regardless of what social-science research was telling us about sex roles and sex-appropriate behaviors, the Patricks and the Maureens and many of the mommies and many of the daddies were simply not paying attention. The social-science literature and psychologists and psychiatrists in particular were concentrating on the difficulties of combining roles of wife, mother, and employee. The late 1960s were replete with books and articles dealing with role conflict. I wrote some of them myself. While intellectuals were running around looking at problems, women (and their men) were out solving or at least combating those problems. But, first, let's look at the prevalent literature of the 1960s.

Outmoded Concepts of Masculinity and Femininity

Let us begin with an apologia for most social-science research. Psychologists and sociologists usually concentrate their efforts on obtaining a sample from the nearest and easiest population. Since most social scientists are academics, what better subject population than beginning Psychology 101 or Sociology 101 students? You walk into a classroom, give out a questionnaire, analyze the results, and immediately reach brilliant conclusions. And so it was in the fifties and the sixties. We drew up lists of adjectives and actions and attitude scales and asked the subjects to rate them as "masculine" or "feminine." Words like "aggression" were termed masculine and "caring" feminine. So we arrived at a picture of what common-sense masculinity and femininity were all about.

One interesting piece of research, by Inge Broverman and her associates, focused on a group of male and female mental-health professionals including social workers, psychiatrists, and psychologists. The subjects were divided into three groups and asked to pick out those adjectives that described a healthy, mature, socially competent (1) man, (2) woman, or (3) adult (no sex specified). The results indicated that a "healthy" adult or a "healthy" man was aggressive, independent, not emotional, adventurous, self-confident. However, a "healthy" woman compared to a "healthy" man was less independent, less adventurous, more easily influenced, more talkative, more excitable in minor crises, more emotional, and more conceited. Broverman writes that these adjectives seem "a most unusual way of describing any mature, healthy individual." More and more research concentrated on "male" and "female" behaviors. And most of the really important research used predominantly male subjects.

Need Achievement

David McClelland and his associates, at Harvard, concentrated their efforts on some exciting research dealing with "need achievement." McClelland and his fellow researchers tried to investigate what family-background characteristics, ethnic background, or sociocultural milieu produced a person who wanted to succeed. They found that the need achiever works well without supervision, works well alone, sets reasonable limits (based on his abilities), likes to control his own destiny, and dislikes failures. The need achiever builds bridges, is a titan of industry, a captain of commerce, and usually (almost always, at least in the laboratory) is *male*. McClelland's research delineated the need achiever and showed us that an encouraging family with a nurturant and ambitious father produced a success-oriented son. Unfortunately, McClelland's research was very fuzzy regarding need achievement of women. Matina Horner decided to see if she could analyze the reasons why women did not seem to succeed as much as did men. Horner developed the concept of "fear of success" and tested it with college-student subjects. She concluded that women did not want to succeed, because those very attributes of success—competition and aggression—which were masculine, were devalued in women. Thus women avoided success in order to "get along with" their male counterparts. While Horner's research is interesting and has provided some provocative leads in sex-role research, it is very difficult to replicate and may indeed be a product of the life and times of the early 1960s. Somehow, for most of the sex-role research on masculinity and femininity, the data simply did not fit real life.

New Psychological Breakthroughs

Psychologists—in particular such women psychologists as Sandra Bem and Janet Spence—became increasingly frustrated at a strict division between masculinity and femininity. Sandra Bem stated in a *Psychology Today* article that she had always felt both masculine *and* feminine. Thus

Bem, Spence, Robert Helmreich, and others began to look into the concept of men and women who were *both* masculine and feminine. Since most research envisages sex roles as two separate isolates, women are supposedly nurturant, loving, and kind. Men are aggressive, forthright, demanding, and competitive. And those are the good adjectives for men, managers, and leaders. The new research deals with men and women who are both loving and aggressive.

The person may have the "good" "masculine" traits and the "good" "feminine" traits. "Good" means "socially approved." For example, "bad" "masculine" traits are expressed with such adjectives as "cruel" and "ruthless." And "bad" "feminine" by "emotional" and "excitable." I put quotation marks around the words "masculine" and "feminine" to show that this is the common-sense or regularly accepted way of describing men and women—even though it is inaccurate. Now, the person who is competitive, loving, aggressive, stable, kind, and nurturant is high in both "masculine" and "feminine" traits. Thus we have a semantic problem on our hands. The researchers turned to the Greeks to find a word to describe not a neuter (or sexless) personality but one who *combines* masculinity and femininity. This person or personality is thus called "androgynous."

Androgyny is a horrible word and conjures up images of a new disease or something that itches a lot. But it is a brilliant concept and fits the real world. Anyone who has been witness to the infighting at the Junior League or the Machiavellian machinations of the League of Women Voters knows perfectly well that women can be hard-driving, success-oriented, competitive, and often ruthless. Books, articles, and professional reputations were built on describing role conflict, Electra complexes, and problems associated with women in male occupations. But the fact was the women *were* in those occupations. Roslyn Willett described the difficulties of being a woman in a man's world: a woman advertising executive. Alice Rossi outlined the lives of women engineers and scientists. More and more women flooded the universities in the 1960s and 1970s. And in other parts of the world women were not anathema, unadjusted, or suffering from role conflict.

Women in Latin America

Even if you didn't buy Betty Friedan's analysis of a Madison Avenue plot or the feminine mystique, obviously American women were not as emancipated as we pretended to be. While only 6 per cent of our doctors are women, over 40 per cent in England, 70 per cent in the Soviet Union, and 30 per cent in Argentina and Chile are women. I became intrigued with these kinds of statistics, and since I had been a Spanish-language major, I wanted to study the phenomenon of women in Latin America.

Once again, my research showed that reality did not fit real life. Since most researchers in Latin America—both Latins and North Americans—were predominantly male, their writings reflected a masculine and myopic view of male-female relationships. The usual, stereotypical view of Latin American women is a quiet, docile mama who leaves home only to go to mass, the forever-faithful and long-suffering wife who endures her husband's peccadillos, or the constantly chaperoned daughter. These types are as extinct as the dodo bird, if indeed they ever existed.

Matriarchy is alive and well in slums and villages. Strong-willed and firm-minded women control their homes and their destinies with a vengeance. Because women do not want to be bound to only one man and because the legal system of Latin America usually gives the husband power of attorney over the wife, most lower-class women purposely avoid the entanglement of marriage. They do need men—but not always the same man. Once the current man has failed in his support of the woman or her family, out he goes. She searches for another man. Or maybe she stays with a man forever and ever but never bothers to marry him.

While machismo exists as braggadocio among the lower classes, it is more a myth among the middle and upper classes. Matriarchs rule their roosts with heavy hands. Sons accede to their mothers' wishes, as also do the daughters-in-law. While family ties are strong and attachments are formed on the basis of the mother, that does not mean that women are solely within the home sphere. In Latin America there is a long-standing tradition of educating women. In fact, spinster lady Protestant schoolteachers from Massachusetts and the U.S. Middle West founded the school systems of Argentina and Chile. The first woman university graduate in Argentina was a medical doctor, Cecilia Grierson, who received her degree in 1889.

One third of the lawyers, over 20 per cent of the doctors, 50 per cent of the dentists, and 20 per cent of the veterinarians in Argentina are women. Unlike the women of the United States in the 1950s, who retreated from office and laboratory to the kitchen, Argentine women graduate in ever-increasing numbers into "male" professions.

I went to Argentina to investigate downtrodden and unhappy women in a *macho* society who were miserable juggling multiple roles. I tried to find out why these women were unhappy and tried to fit my results into a straitjacket of 1950s U.S. role-conflict sociology. It just didn't work: these women in "male" professions were remarkably well adjusted. I developed a host of explanations to show why these women did not experience this role conflict. These reasons included general approval of women's education, a long tradition of female employment, maternity benefits including pre- and postnatal care, free hospitalization, free layette, payment of salary during maternity leave, use and availability of domestic servants, husband's approval, and peer support. Some women mentioned that they had some difficulties working with men, but they also had problems with some of their sister professionals. As was to be expected, the more women in a given profession the less the role strain, the less aberrant the woman, and the more she could adapt to her professional, wifely, and maternal roles. Few women mentioned prejudice against women. The women centered their complaints on the general instability of Argentina, such as galloping inflation, constant changes of government, lack of research funds, and poor working conditions. My respondents taught me more social science than I had ever learned before. Women professionals dragged me through hospitals, slums, laboratories, and law courts. They spent hours lecturing me on how one of the richest nations in the world had degenerated into a country with understaffed hospitals, badly equipped classrooms, harassed researchers, and professionals who wanted only to emigrate. I met revolutionaries and oligarchs. I did not meet downtrodden women who felt put upon because of their sex. Therein began my interest in female coping rather than in female "problems."

Granted, Argentina is in a somewhat unique situation in Latin America. Argentina is a nation of white second- and third-generation Europeans, a country of casual Roman Catholics where one quarter of the university graduates are of Jewish background and whose major city, Buenos Aires, is a sybarite's delight. Buenos Aires is a cosmopolitan city of theaters, bookstalls, boutiques, culinary delights, opera, and literary conceits. Buenos Aires *literati* speak unaccented French, and the city has the highest ratio of psychiatrists to general population in the world. But while Argentina is distinct from most nations in Latin America, it is still a Spanish/Italian country, where one ought to—on the basis of male social-science literature—expect the women to still flit around in mantillas and pray a lot.

Mantillas are reserved for special occasions. Since women constitute a large portion of every profession, I started taking stock of my women respondents. These women were harassed and harried, but no more so than their male counterparts. Interestingly, most of the women took special pains to emphasize their femininity. Since Buenos Aires is a city of fashion, boutiques, hairdressers, masseuses, and dressmakers, middle- and upper-class women are madly interested in fashion and style. Once a dress appears in a Paris salon, you can guarantee that the same pattern will be seen within weeks on the streets of Buenos Aires. Women doctors, lawyers, and dentists in

Buenos Aires reflected this intense devotion to high style. The women respondents in my sample were invariably well dressed, manicured, and coiffed in the ultra-chic latest whatever. No matter how small an office these women might have, they made some effort to personalize it with plants, paintings, or photographs of their children.

Just as these women emphasized their femininity in their dress and their offices, so also did they use feminine wiles to get their own way. Rather than assuming a "masculine" appearance and masculine behavior, they would use any feminine trick or wile to accomplish a task. I observed these well-educated women coaxing, wheedling, flirting, using baby talk, and occasionally crying in order to obtain some result. Beneath a façade of helplessness, there lurked ruthless, calculating creatures. I found their behavior insidious and fascinating. Another kind of reality might have been painted by a traditional observer who felt these women to be presumptuous and abnormal—greedy, because they wanted male success and female fulfillment. Admittedly, these Argentine professional women were Machiavellian creatures who manipulated their environment with skill, flair, and cunning. They survived. And they still had a sense of humor.

Back to the United States

The question still haunted me, though: why and how did these women in a supposedly male-dominated society manage with such verve, while American women were marching, protesting, organizing, and bemoaning their fate at every turn? The answer was that there was a social revolution in process. And since I was a part of that social revolution, I never even noticed it. The dismal, sick, anti-woman fifties were being turned around. For example, in 1955, 6 per cent of medical-school graduates were women; in 1970, 9 per cent; in 1975, 15 per cent; and in 1978, over 24 per cent of medical students are women. In 1955, a scarce 0.4 per cent of all law school graduates were women, and by 1975, the percentage of women graduates had increased only to 3.5 per cent—but there were increases. In the mid sixties, my own field of sociology was a weird anomaly. Even though 60 per cent of the bachelor's degrees were granted to women, thus making sociology a feminine field, only 30 per cent of the master's degrees and a scant 15 per cent of the doctorates were granted to women. There obviously were self-selection, some prejudice, a lot of bad counseling, and the feminine mystique at work among women sociologists. However, by 1975, 31 per cent of the doctorates in sociology were granted to women. The feminine mystique was changing to a feminine prerequisite. Equal opportunity and a new ideology were at work.

However, there was still a dichotomy between the silent social revolution and the mass media. New magazines such as *Ms.* appeared, and their instant success gave pause to *Ladies' Home Journal* and *McCall's*. Editorial boards and publishers soon woke up to the fact that magazines and advertisers should speak to the working woman. So the ads told the working woman that she could have a career—whatever it might be, from file clerk to telephone lineman to naval officer to head of a law firm—and still be a beautiful and a charming hostess. So began the instant revolution. Instant potatoes. Instant pudding. Instant, no-mix cakes.

Microwave ovens. Crock-pots. Instant weight loss. Do-it-yourself divorce kits.

Slowly television and the movies discovered the new woman. There was no mass rush back to the Rosalind Russell and Bette Davis heroines, but some sensitive movies and a few television plays showed the dilemma of the woman caught between traditional mores and an ideology concerning self-fulfillment. Miss Clairol and Tang capitalized on the new image of the glamorous lady doctor. A new myth developed: the super women who do all the super things. Dashing around town in Gucci shoes with a Vuitton briefcase, the new woman attends her daughter's graduation from ballet school, drops in on her son's cub-scout meeting, and then casually cooks a dinner for thirty people. The new myth is almost as enslaving as the old one of *Kinder-Küche-Kirche*—even with *The Joy of Cooking*. What happens to those women who do devote themselves to career and home? What kind of price do they pay? Is there any kind of price that any woman has to pay? Are there new styles of acting and behaving that accrue to woman and by example or success to men also? Before we can answer that question, it is necessary to have a quick look at some important findings in management, supervision, leadership, and business administration.

4

New Women
and the New
Management Styles

MANAGEMENT science began with Elton Mayo's famous study on the Hawthorne plant of the Western Electric Company, in 1927. Mayo and his associates found that workers were very sensitive to the demands and needs of their peers and the attitudes that supervisors exhibited toward them. Most managers had assumed that money was the ONLY important variable in motivating people to work. Of course, some managers then and now are convinced that the *stick* approach—i.e., threats of layoffs, reductions in force, and outright wholesale firing—will have the same kind of motivating effect. And sometimes it does. However, as an outgrowth of the Hawthorne studies, researchers found that workers moved and maneuvered in their workplace according to peer-group norms. For example, in factories people shouldn't work too fast or too slow. The work group set the norm—not the foreman or the time-management person in the main office. Work breaks, style of life, recreational facilities, a sense of belonging to an organization—all these variables were (and are) important to increase production or at least maintain production at a high level. Organizational theorists began to study the differences between blue-collar and white-collar workers. They sought answers or solutions as to the best managerial style.

McGregor's idea of Theory X and Theory Y gained popularity in the 1960s. McGregor dubbed a leadership style consisting of acting in a terrorizing, authoritarian manner Theory X. Given research on workers and supervisors, Theory X was inefficient and useless as a managerial tool. Theory Y, on the other hand, worked. Theory Y accepts the basic dignity of the human spirit. The Theory Y manager involves his workers in decisions. Theory Y managers are flexible and are interested in the needs, aspirations, problems, and intellectual capabilities of employees. Of course, McGregor's theory assumes that the manager recognizes that his employees are rational human beings who seek responsibility.

Abraham Maslow built on McGregor's theory and expanded the idea of man (and woman) as a self-actualizing creature. Maslow drew up what he called a hierarchy of needs. He said that once basic needs (or an upward-spiraling curve of needs) were met, then workers could reach the ideal of self-actualization. For example, a hungry, tired man working in a dangerous job is concerned with primary needs, and his intellectual goal of self-actualization doesn't enter into his intellectual framework. Maslow's hierarchy of needs is as follows: First of all, man must satisfy *physiological needs*, of food, water, warmth, shelter. Then he must meet *safety needs*, such as protection from injury or danger on the job. Next there is a social need for *belongingness and love*. There is thus a need to give and to receive love and a basic need of belonging to a group. Next there is a *need for esteem*. Every individual has a need to be held in respect by others and to be granted some status. The final need is a *growth need*: the *need for self-actualization*. This is the creative need, the desire to become something better, to realize creative needs.

Frederick Herzberg built on Maslow's hierarchy of needs and refined or made more explicit those needs that have to be fulfilled before the process of self-actualization can begin. Herzberg wrote that workers must have their "hygiene factors" (e.g., good working conditions) fulfilled before they can go on to the important motivators such as a sense of accomplishment through the job. Herzberg pointed out that *job enrichment* is a growth motivator. Hence the recent emphasis on job enrichment and job enlargement.

Since 1932, Rensis Likert has focused his research on groups, and he, too, emphasizes the humane side of human organizations. Likert states that there are four kinds of leadership style:

System 1—Exploitive-Authoritative
System 2—Benevolent-Authoritative
System 3—Consultative
System 4—Participative-Group.

Not too surprisingly, given the intellectual ethos of managerial science, Likert opts for System 4, the Participative-Group. He contends that a System 4 company is creative and has high production.

Throughout the 1960s and 1970s, based on McGregor, Herzberg, Maslow, and Likert, business schools, case studies, and reams of managerial texts have emphasized the caring, nurturant, involved, aggressive, and competent leadership style. Robert Blake and Judith Mouton tried to introduce the concept of task and managerial style in their "Managerial Grid," with magic numbers like 1, 1 and 5, 5 and 9, 1 and associated differences in styles and production results. More and more jargon was added to the language. However, laboratory results and observations in real-life situations seemed to bear out the *humane* approach of management.

No matter how you slice most of the management-leadership-industry-sociology-psychology literature of the past twenty years, you get the same kind of profile. The best leader in most situations is one who is high in task orientation and high in personal relationships. Someone who pounds on his subordinates and does not care for his employees' feelings and needs is not necessarily a good manager. On the other hand, a leader who is so busy taking care of the personal problems and troubles of his/her subordinates that the *job* doesn't get done is a lousy manager. He/she may be a super boss to have, but this manager, in turn, is a terrible employee to his/her boss.

But the highly nurturant and highly task-oriented personality that comes to us from the management research sounds remarkably familiar, like the Spence/Bem/Helmreich androgynous personality. Androgynous people are high in aggression and high in nurturance. It is to be hoped that they are high in competence as well. Spence and Helmreich write in their recent (1978) book on masculinity and femininity that competence is more often than not associated with an androgynous personality.

So the new management style fits the new concept of masculinity and femininity. Neither one of these concepts is particularly new, but their marriage in management literature may be. But perhaps we ought to backtrack a little and return to the traditional view of femininity.

Kindness and Caring

While the classical sex-role division of maleness and femaleness is markedly unfair, such stereotypical thinking had a base in historical fact. Women were child bearers who fed, nursed, educated, and cared for young children. Not by virtue of "natural" ability but because society forced women into the role of educator and nurse, these characteristics accrued to women. It is interesting to note sex-role reversals among saints: Francis of Assisi manifested "feminine" characteristics, while Teresa of Ávila was decidedly masculine. Or were they both androgynous? Historians recount how Florence Nightingale and Clara Barton raised the status of nursing. Books tell of the gentle lady with a lamp and the brave, lonely woman on the battlefield and somehow do not emphasize their tough, competitive, aggressive, and highly masculine behavior. Or were those two women also androgynous?

There are no yes-or-no answers. However, nurturance and aggression are not uncomplementary characteristics among our forebears.

Men, too, are taught to be kind and loving. Fathers, as well as mothers, kiss bruises and put on Band-Aids. Unfortunately, hugs and kisses come more often from mothers than from fathers. Children know that they can climb up on Mommy's knee easier than Daddy's. Boys learn that kisses are "yucky," even though they secretly long for some physical reassurance. We steel our men to contain their emotions.

No wonder, then, that we have a host of therapists and organizational consultants trying to "unfreeze" male emotions. Large corporations devote personnel-training and executive-development sessions ranging from a few days to sixteen weeks to train mid- and upper-level managers to become more "people oriented." Schools of industrial management are teaching (primarily male) students to be highly relationship-oriented management supervisors. The people-ness in this equation adds up to the traditional view of femininity or femaleness. Kindly behavior, caring attitudes, nurturant personalities—these are what we traditionally call "feminine" characteristics. The kind of socialization that women get—by virtue of playing with dolls, crying a little, giving vent to emotions, listening to other people's troubles—is now valuable in the marketplace.

Alice in Businessland

So, again, we have a distorted mirror of acceptable behavior. Even though men are supposedly socialized to be aggressive and competitive, they are also expected to be caring and nurturant. Yet women seem to think that in order to be successes in the male business world, they must be aggressive, competitive, and non-nurturant. If you glance through some of the more radical rhetoric of the 1960s women's movement, you will find that most women's liberationist writing extolled the virtues of machismo and denigrated the classical womanly qualities of gentleness and tenderness.

Women professionals often assume that they have to stop being "female" and become cruel, tough, vindictive, and ruthless men. Therein lies the problem. Young women students fall prey to this false ideology and say that they want to maintain their femininity and refuse to become men. Then they opt for high school science teaching (an acceptable combination of nurturance and "maleness"), rather than engineering. When a woman does move into management or supervisory positions, and if she adopts all the male characteristics associated with ruthless ambition, she fulfills another stereotype: a bitchy, castrating female.

Fortunately, not all women are doing so. Many women have discovered that femininity in the business world is a decided asset. What we call "feminine" can contribute to a more harmonious workplace. It may be that highly educated professional women have a decided advantage over men of similar education and social class. That is, the women's liberation movement is more liberating to women than to men. Even though all sorts of disclaimers are made to the effect that the women's movement is meant to free men as well as women, maybe women are getting more of the good things from their childhood socialization and their increased educational opportunities. For example, I wrote about the fact that chemistry and Erector sets are now acceptable toys for girls but dolls still are somewhat ambiguous gifts for boys. It's fine for girls to take shop in high school, but boys die a thousand deaths when forced to take home economics. Until our young boys learn to dress and undress doll babies and mix brownies with aplomb, androgynous males will be in short supply.

Yet our women are receiving messages every day that they can be doctors, lawyers, captains of industry, and titans of commerce. From the increased numbers of women entering and graduating from hitherto exclusively all-male bastions, there are indeed more and more androgynous women around. And judging from feature stories in newspapers and magazines, few of this new breed "sacrifice" their femininity. The professional woman usually was portrayed as a stodgy creature wearing a suit made out of porcupine quills; she wore flat, "sensible" shoes and had her hair cut by a local barber. She was a masculinized or horribly neutered female with no hormones or flowing juices. Contrast today's busy young professional woman. She is well dressed, is a sexual creature, and is very competent. Her power plays and ploys are decidedly masculine and her clothes strictly from Vogue magazine. I interviewed several highly successful young women who pointed out that the feminine woman can manipulate in a masculine world very well indeed. I was and am delighted to find that my competent, coping Argentine professional women have equally charming and efficient sisters in the United States.

Be Nice to the Squirrels

One of these competent women is a good friend of mine who agreed to let me interview her over a diet lunch of carrot sticks and yoghurt. We sat in her large office with a breathtaking view of the Manhattan skyline, and I felt like Mimi's country cousin from the hinterlands. Mimi is a quiet, birdlike little woman who controls many millions of dollars in contracts for a very, very large multinational corporation. She is living testimony to the success of equal opportunity. Mimi began working in the contracts division of XYZ Corporation right out of a business administration B.A. from Purdue University. She had one desk out of a whole line of desks in a huge bullpen area. She shared a miserable apartment with two other equally miserable girls from the Midwest who had come to Manhattan to seek fame, fortune, and a husband. Mimi enrolled in a night-school course for a master's in business administration and began to bone up on contract law and in particular the strange provisos relating to equal opportunity. When her firm finally woke up to the fact that they needed a specialist in that particular area, they were delighted that they could promote from within the corporation, and Mimi's brains and talent were richly rewarded.

Mimi has never forgotten how and why she rose to the top so quickly. During my lunchtime sojourn with her, she expounded on her management philosophy.

"Someday I am going to find time to make a needlepoint of my own personal motto," she proclaimed. "I'm going to hang it on the wall. It will say, 'Be Nice to the Squirrels.'"

When I asked who and what were the squirrels, Mimi continued at length:

A good executive is only as good as his or her aides, secretaries, assistants, and researchers. You learn very early in any organizational game that the squirrels make treadmills go around in psychological experiments and make a corporate enterprise work. Robert Townsend writes in his *Up the Organization* that the most important person in any business is the girl who answers the telephone. She makes or breaks customer goodwill. Well, that really goes for little people of all kinds and types as well. Be nice to the squirrels in this order: janitors, secretaries, assistants, and aides. Never, never confuse titles with power. When you are on your way up, learn that your own contemporaries will someday have a great deal of power. Today's assistant clerk may be tomorrow's President. Also, the power brokers are secretaries who make appointments and who can refuse to put your telephone calls through. Rudeness and lack of courtesy will always come back to haunt you.

Caring is what makes the corporate enterprise work. So you don't want to go to your secretary's daughter's wedding. Go. So you don't want to drag yourself halfway across town to your assistant's father's funeral. Go. You may not have time to stay, but the fact that you went and paid some respect to one of your employees will be repaid a thousand times.

Being nice isn't necessarily female, it's just being nice. I think that I was so badly treated as a young-woman-recent-graduate in that god-awful bullpen, that I remember those few people who were kind to me in the beginning years. Luckily I didn't get poisoned by the mistreatment but only resolved *never* to repeat that kind of behavior when I became a boss.

Mimi, of course, never doubted that she would become a success, either in the XYZ Corporation or somewhere else. She is the classic example of Alice Rossi's professional pioneer.

Alice Rossi's 1965 study of women in male professions presents a profile of reasonably well-adjusted women who were more often than not only children or eldest children. They came from homes with highly educated parents, and in particular the father was a kindly, loving parent who took a deep interest in the daughter's education and aspirations. Mimi also is the product of a private, all-girl school where she exercised the same kind of leadership that she showed as a student at Purdue. Even though she was one of the few women at the business/management school, she was confident because she had parental encouragement and her own sense of security in her self-worth. Mimi didn't worry about being a success; she simply accepted that it would come because she was good. And she was and is a very good person to boot.

Christina's Ethic

Like Mimi, Christina also lives by a nurturant ethic, but she is probably more calculating than Mimi. Christina is a high-ranking researcher who cuts effectively through bureaucratic Mickey Mouse. Christina's hard-working, fiercely devoted staff is a rarity in a company renowned for its cutthroat reputation. She and I talked at length in her Spartan office, situated in a corner of a long, narrow laboratory:

Supervising a research-and-design staff is like being a ringmaster among temperamental tigers. Every person in this lab has a couple of degrees from fine schools and an easily bruised and exceptionally large ego. They are all prima donnas and most of them have the emotional maturity of three-year-olds. Maybe that's why I am the first person to control this maniacal group of egomaniacs. I raised two children and am used to dealing with infantile reactions. I believe in the sound management principle of good working conditions and excellent salaries. But my mad scientists work for professional recognition and a pat on the head.

The last person to supervise this lab was an absolute disaster, because he never recognized the subtleties of dealing with highly educated, creative people. Harold [the previous supervisor] thought that money and an occasional trip to a European conference was enough to mollify his staff. It didn't work that way at all. I got this job not because I was so terrifically good but because Harold was so terribly bad. He had over 50 per cent turnover in one six-month period. Now, take a look around this lab and remember that there isn't a person here who is earning less than twenty-five thousand dollars a year. Of course, some people could earn more other places, but on the whole the salaries are competitive with the going rate for chemical researchers throughout the United States. So money is not the reason why people stay or go. They stay with me because I use the same principles with my mad scientists as I do with my clerical help: recognition. That is the key.

Since everyone assumed that a doctorate makes you somehow different from the rest of the world, the previous supervisors never bothered to give out the little goodies that make the rest of the staff happy: pins; promotions;

certificates of appreciation; little luncheons; an occasional bonus for a job well done. The secretaries AND the research scientists all need those ego boosts. As a matter of fact, I think that my mad scientists have such thin ego defenses that they need the continual reassurance of a job well done even more than the less-educated personnel.

Christina then went on to show how her part of the company differed from the other divisions:

This company is famous for its ruthless operations. They are learning that they can't step on people and destroy them, because it's bad personnel policy. But they're learning *very* slowly. The old-style supervisors in this company suffer from congenital paranoia. Anyone who looks good or who shows some creative ability or who is a young man on the make is quickly given the heave ho. We now have a new chairman of the board, and he is trying to reverse these tendencies but will never accomplish the job until he fires or converts every one of these dodos.

My policy has always been that if you have a talented, creative person in your work group, give him (or her) a free rein. Of course, you have to learn to cover your ass as well. If your creative genius falls flat on his butt, you can come through with a Pontius Pilate act. If the young genius comes through with a new widget, you are covered in glory. You claim fame because you hired the genius and let him (her) perform his own wizardry. The subordinate gets all the credit for a terrific job—and by osmosis so does the supervisor. Most important of all: you never, ever steal from a subordinate. If you are talented and creative yourself, you have no reason to fear subordinates who are equally or even more talented than you. The secret of good management is to take your coterie of good people with you as you advance up the corporate ladder. You have to be prepared to fight for rewards for your own people. Those rewards are promotions, extra bonuses, rugs on the floor, or advanced education. You'd be surprised at the number of advanced degrees in this department that are the direct result of my hounding the personnel-development people into letting my clerks or secretaries take extra courses. Very few people seem to understand that my staff is loyal to me because I am loyal to them.

Christina then suggested that I talk to some of her people in the laboratory. She left the laboratory and didn't come back for several hours and I wandered around talking to some of the "mad geniuses." It was true they were fiercely loyal, but each one in his or her own way had reason to believe that Christina was committed not only to the laboratory organization but to every person in that division. Christina's management style may only be appropriate to a group of some fifty people or endemic to a reasearch-and-design division. Her very personal and somewhat maternal style may be instigated only face to face and by a middle-level supervisor. I think not. If the same principles apply on mid level, they should apply on upper level as well. The upper-level manager has to ask his (her) subordinates the constant question, "What have you done for your people today (this week) (this month)?" Of course, the initial problem is to get the upper-level job.

The Beautiful Lady Lawyer

Rosie is part of a new Washington breed of glamorous and very influential young lady lawyers. Rosie began her career fresh out of a prestigious Ivy League school and joined a very prestigious and very male New York City firm. She soon learned that she had been hired primarily because the firm was under the equal-opportunity gun and she was truly a token female. Not only that, male or female, her problems were compounded by being young. Rosie had enough sense to realize that it would take her years and years to advance within the firm—and sex was not the discriminating variable. She wangled a mid-level attorney's job in a federal regulatory agency and soon advanced to important policy-making jobs and even sooner to several promotions with other agencies.

Rosie and I see each other often, and I asked her permission to interview her. She was pleased and said her management secret was that every woman within or out of government and within or out of industry needed a sponsor.

She contends that most men and *all* women need a mentor for guidance, advice, sponsorship, and often protection. It's hard to find a mentor if you graduate from a midwestern or a Podunk school. The Ivy League or Stanford types are inbred and are part of a close coterie. The old-boy network is still predominantly male, but daughters and daughters-in-law are breaking into the network. Just as the extended-kin network of the Argentine upper-class society, so also is the Eastern Seaboard admitting women to its inhouse ranks. She admits that it's a kind of paternalism, but Rosie says, "Better paternalism than outright discrimination."

Rosie contends that she doesn't give a sweet damn about behaving like a man. She is the daughter of a lawyer, and when I introduced her to the concept of androgyny she was intrigued.

> I suppose I never really worried about my femininity and my brains being in conflict. My father naturally assumed that I would become a lawyer. My mother naturally assumed that I would always be well dressed and well groomed. Probably the worst period of their lives was when I was in law school and running around in blue jeans and a fatigue jacket. I thought it was awfully tacky at the time, but I had to fit in with the rest of the mid-sixties crowd. Now you can't even get me near blue jeans, even for a country weekend!

Rosie has a beautiful townhouse and a live-in boy friend. The boy friend/lover/housemate is a well-to-do banker who wants to get married and can't persuade Rosie to make their illicit union licit.

Sex, Love, and Marriage Aren't the Same Thing

Rosie and her contemporaries have a somewhat *laissez-faire* attitude toward marriage. Gone are the days of the frantic rush to the altar in your senior year. New attitudes toward sexual morality, effective methods of contraception, and a hedonistic attitude toward sex all stymie the frantic hormonal push to get married. In my virginal high school days, nice girls "didn't," and now nice girls "do." If there is a relief of sexual tension and no need to worry about untoward or out-of-wedlock conception, marriage becomes somewhat extraneous. This new morality impacts on the workplace as well.

The rather simplistic explanation that most male managers would offer in order to justify their NOT hiring women in important positions had some basis in fact: women did get pregnant at awkward times, did leave their jobs, and often did not return. Now with pregnancies planned—at least among upper- and middle-class, college-educated women—the birth rate has taken a sudden and dramatic dip. Childless couples are extremely common. Childless and married women are accepting and fulfilling responsible jobs. By law employers are forbidden to ask women about their plans for pregnancy or their birth control. I well remember job interviews in the sixties, when I had to bite my lip in fury as I was quizzed regarding the kind of birth control I used and did I have any immediate plans to become (or was I already) pregnant. But I had to suffer whatever humiliation or insult came my way. Equal opportunity didn't exist, and I desperately needed those jobs.

Times changed and much for the better. The 1960 government approval of the birth-control pill freed women from untoward or at least unplanned pregnancies. Abortion on demand meant that women did not have to endure unwanted pregnancies—if their contraception had failed. The impact on women workers was profound. Women could and did remain childless. Or they planned one or two pregnancies at their (and their profession's) convenience.

Take teaching, for example. Not only did the birth rate drop enormously, which meant that fewer and fewer teachers were needed, but more teachers *stayed* in the teaching profession. Prior to the pill, teaching was an "in-and-out" profession. That is, women taught for a few years, became pregnant, went home to take care of the baby, and came back part or full time several years later. Or they worked only as substitutes. Or never returned at all. When more and more women began to take the pill, fewer and fewer women teachers left the profession. All those women teachers who "stayed in," plus a drop in the birth rate, meant that recently graduated teachers had no jobs and drove taxicabs or waited on tables. Such is life for the teaching profession.

However, for the middle- and upper-level manager and supervisor, freedom from unwanted or unplanned pregnancies was extraordinary. Now because of the birth-control pill, there was absolutely no reason why male managers and supervisors could feebly protest that it wasn't worthwhile to hire a woman, who would stay only a few years.

Androgyny Among the Men

However, we noticed feminine reactions among younger men. Many of them were job hoppers and job changers; they stayed only a few years too. These very problems that were supposedly endemic to the female seemed to be the same for mid- and upper-level male managers as well.

Nonetheless, as the sixties progressed, more and more organizational specialists focused on some ephemeral variable called "quality of life." If workers were not motivated solely by money, and if status awards such as larger and larger offices were no longer important, what was? Men who began to rise to the middle and upper levels apparently were more concerned with their families' welfare than with the company ethos. The company man was fast disappearing. No one has really investigated this phenomenon thoroughly enough, and I can only make a few guesses regarding men's and women's attitudes toward the emerging 1970s work ethic. While work *is* important, self-fulfillment, in Maslow's or Herzberg's terms, comes not only from work but also from the family. As these men and women in their thirties take a look at their predecessors in their forties and fifties, they begin to take stock of the emotional and psychological price for success: alcoholic wives, children who are dropouts or hippies or drug freaks, rising divorce rate, heart attacks, cirrhosis of the liver, ulcers—the list goes on and on.

Apparently there is a dreadful cost to rising to the top, and many women and men refuse to assume the burden. Companies that regularly move their employees every few years now have troubles, first, attracting, and then, keeping their mid-level people. Moving is traumatic for all family members. Men cannot drag their children from school to school and interrupt a wife's career or advanced education, and still expect the family to remain intact and unscarred. Notice that up to now I have referred to "men" who refuse to go along with every whim and vagary of their respective companies. That is because most supervisors are men and the recent revolt by mid-level executives is relatively rare.

Prior to the 1970s, another epithet hurled at women executives was that their wife/mother role interfered with their executive role. Now we realize that a good percentage of a man's stability or instability comes from his home environment. Perhaps women were more likely to express their problems and feelings to their peers and supervisors. But men suffer dislocation and longing just as women do.

Watch a man who has a seriously ill child or who is undergoing a traumatic divorce. His performance is hardly up to par. He will not be the best possible employee. All the same criticisms lobbed against women employees can be levied at the male. Some men (and obviously some women) can compartmentalize their personal and professional lives. Few do. Few can.

With increasing emphasis on personal relationships within the office and nurturance on the part of the supervisor and trust on the part of employees and peers, personal lives and professional lives are intertwined. Not only that, but with more women working or returning to school, more men have to accept the nurturant-parent role of taking children to and from dental and doctor appointments. Ferrying kids around town is now male work and not just woman's work. Actually the single-parent *father* is a new and growing phenomenon.

As it has become more and more acceptable for fathers to be nurturant and loving, so is it acceptable for men to fight for custody of their children. As we understand the nature of masculinity/femininity and realize that maternal instincts are few and far between, judges grant custody to the single-parent father. Maybe we will have more child-care facilities in office and factory because of the single-parent father rather than the single-parent mother. So another criticism against women bites the dust.

Feminine Women in Masculine Jobs

If the new supervisor is more nurturant, or what we call "feminine," and if women are genetically, psychologically, or sociologically more inclined toward this nurturant behavior, the women should be better or at least excellent supervisors. The new leadership style is really not feminine but masculine-feminine. For those women who graduate in business administration, law, medicine, architecture, or any of the so-called "masculine" fields, the future is bright. If French lady lawyers and Argentine women dentists and Chilean lady judges and English women doctors can cope, why can't American women? Maybe we are only now catching up with the rest of the world.

But sometimes there is a dreadful cost in anxiety, tension, and illness for those women who are unable to accept their androgynous roles. Or maybe those women who have been socialized to a feminine role and thrust into masculine work worlds pay a greater price. Let us now turn to the dark side: role conflict and role confusion.

5

Stress, Health, and Disease

From Witch to Expert

T HROUGHOUT history, men and women have meditated on the distinction between the body and the mind.
What happens to the mind when the body dies? What is
the soul? What happens to us when we are asleep? Can
the mind cure the body? Can the mind make the body
sick? Myth, legend, story, oral tradition—all posed these
questions. Witches, curers, scribes, prophets, medicine
men—all sought to answer them. Although anthro-
pologists, explorers, and wide-eyed travelers reported such
strange phenomena as voodoo death and walking on coals,

their stories were airily dismissed by pragmatic armchair theorists as so much hogwash. Today, the questions remain the same. Yesterday's shamans and seers have been replaced by "experts," who are providing new answers to these age-old questions. Let's look at what some of them have to say.

Good Stress: Eustress

Hans Selye, of McGill University, in Montreal, Canada, is the world's foremost expert on stress. In fact, Selye introduced the concept of stress into the physiological-medical literature. However, Selye is very careful to point out that there is a distinction between "good stress" and "bad stress." That is, all living is a stressful activity. "Good stress," or what Selye likes to call "eustress," is the excitement that we feel for a job promotion, graduation from high school, the senior prom, one's wedding, or moving to a luxurious new home. These are stressful activities. They do not rank as high on the Holmes and Rahe scale as "bad stress," such as a divorce or death of a spouse, but all exciting, depressing, hurtful, or enjoyable activities are stressful.

Selye further emphasizes the fact that all organisms need some kind of excitement. Some people need more activity than others—the beach bum versus the corporation executive. Some men break down under stress easier than others. But all people need a little spice and excitement in their lives, otherwise we would live vegetable existences. Dull, uninteresting experiences make dull, listless, and very uninteresting people. Good stress is absolutely necessary for human beings to be physiologically and psychologically fully developed. For example, monkeys raised in isolation are dull, listless, and quite stupid compared to monkeys raised in a cage with monkey brothers and sisters and a monkey mother. World-famous psychologist Harry Harlow has performed many experiments with chimpanzees. Harlow has raised chimpanzees with their real, live, furry, cuddly mothers. And he has raised chimps in isolation, with the baby clinging to a wire-mesh mother substitute, with a bottle lashed to the wire mesh. Chimpanzees raised with the wire-mesh mother substitute are timid, fearful, unsure of how to act, and generally quite bonkers compared to chimps raised with a furry, cuddly, real, live mother.

We can move from chimpanzees and similar studies on rats to people. Children raised in orphanages are more neurotic and more fearful than children raised in home environments. One problem psychologists worry about in regard to hospitalization of children is their isolation from excitement and daily "eustress." Most studies on childhood development emphasize the need for color, books, excitement, conversation, music, noise, and general stimulation of *all* the senses. Man is the original curiosity cat, and we need to constantly foster that curiosity. Simply hanging a mobile over a child's crib contributes to the baby's development of eye movement and perception of shape and color. Walking and falling, laughing at a shadow, reaching for a hot stove—all these actions are part of growing up and part and parcel of stress. Stress is life. Eustress is a good part of life.

We need movement, laughter, joy, rushing, reaching, striving, and a whole brouhaha of noise, color, and activity in order to survive as vibrant, living human beings. While some of us opt for the peace and tranquillity of a monastery, most of us could not stand that lethargy. We are noisy, nosy creatures. Good stress contributes to our psychological well-being. Selye points out that eustress such as exercise, hobbies, outside interests, or a fulfilling job also leads to psychic well-being. If you are stimulated and not overwrought, you are psychologically healthy and correspondingly physically well. On the other hand, bad stress, or the inability to cope with the turmoil of life, leads to some very sad and disheartening results. The jury is still out on this subject. Holmes and Rahe feel that *all* stress— good or bad, pleasant occasions or unhappy ones—lead eventually to the physical deterioration of a person. In other words, if, in one year, you marry, go on a honeymoon, get a job promotion, move to another city, take out a bank loan, and buy a house, you are slated for a serious debilitating illness. Other researchers pooh-pooh the mind-body connection entirely and find only tenuous links between stress events and illness. Still other researchers, such as the biofeedback enthusiasts, go beyond Selye and see all illness and any cures only through the control of mind over body. Medical research has divided into bitter camps regarding the question of immunology and stress reactions.

Stress and Cancer

Medical researchers have sought for years to find a link between disease and stress. One of the best tools is the MMPI (Minnesota Multiphasic Personality Inventory). If you give patients these tests, you can measure their levels of anxiety, pathology, neuroticism, etc. At the same time, you may find a link between disturbed personalities and particular illnesses. Also, researchers ask patients about their life history during the past year. Quite often, patients have recounted a series of highly stressful events such as the death of a parent *and* a divorce *and* financial problems. Sometimes the troubles are more than you can imagine. One of my fellow researchers who continually suffered one year from debilitating flu attacks is just one case. However, he had reason to crawl in bed with the pillows over his head. Within the previous year, his father had died, his father-in-law had had coronary bypass surgery, his house had burned, and the insurance company had fought him over payment for the house repairs. My friend Morry was lucky that he succumbed only to flu, rather than to a small stroke.

But Morry is only a subsample of one. And that, unfortunately, is how most medical researchers work. When I began going through medical literature for data for this book, I was appalled at the lack of statistical care that medical researchers use. Rat physiologists are much more careful than medical doctors. The words reliability and validity don't exist. There is little, if any, worry over sample size. Medical researchers report "breakthroughs" on a sample of *one*. The kind of statistical impropriety that would get a sociologist or psychologist thrown out of his/her profession seems to be everyday business for the medical researchers. However, rats, monkeys, and chimpanzees are much more expendable than human beings. We have laws and ethics governing what kinds of experimentation are permissible on human beings. Nonetheless, doctors sometimes overreach their data.

Such is the inconclusive and conflicting case with cancer and stress. There seems to be some kind of link between painful and disturbing life events and cancer.

Studies from 1946 to 1964 at Johns Hopkins University using extensive interviews and the MMPI show that cancer develops in people who generally are quiet, not aggressive, and emotionally contained. Other studies on cancer-prone patients indicate that women with cancer were highly controlled, very conforming, less assertive, less adventurous, and less spontaneous than those whose cancer tests were negative. Researcher after researcher has found a link between depression, feelings of hopelessness, self-destructive drives (which they call passive suicide), sexual malfunctioning, inability to express hostile feelings, helplessness, and *cancer*. However, once again we are faced with the chicken-and-egg problem. Are these women tense, hopeless, and depressed before they have cancer, or do they have or find out they have cancer and correspondingly become depressed with feelings of hopelessness? Research does indicate that persons suffering from anxiety and depression are more likely to experience the onset of cancer than persons who are not anxious and depressed. In particular, on the life-stress scale developed by Holmes and Rahe, those persons who have suffered the loss of a loved one, whether through death, divorce, or some kind of separation, are also likely to have cancer.

Yet, this kind of research is terribly after-the-fact. The researcher asks a woman with breast cancer what has happened to her in the past year. The patient's mother died and two children left for college; death; separation anxiety; empty-nest syndrome; breast cancer. There is an interesting contrast: what about those women who had a parent die and children leave for school and didn't have cancer? Or, conversely, how many women who developed breast cancer within a given year had no untoward life-stress events? The current state of the art in medical cancer research simply cannot answer these questions. Yet these are the very questions that have to be asked and answered with statistical precision; otherwise we end up playing a terrible game of "blame the victim."

The concept of blaming the victim comes to us through criminology. The victim gets blamed for the crime. The reason the girl was raped was because she wore a miniskirt. The reason the man was robbed was because his car broke down and he was at fault. So also do we see a dangerous tendency for blaming the cancer victim. If a woman cannot withstand stress, she gets cancer. It's her fault and not the concern of the doctor or of medical science. This analogy is very similar to the nineteenth-century, romanticized idea of a tubercular personality. Some people just "naturally" got tuberculosis, in particular artistic or bohemian people. It wasn't until people began to make a link between germs, sputum, bad air, poor sanitary conditions, and all the other evils of fetid city living, that the idea of a tubercular personality fell by the wayside.

Yet there are links between cancer and life stress just as there are links between life stress and heart attacks. Recent and somewhat fuzzy research by biofeedback experts shows that we can make connections with Yoga mind-body control. For example, the biofeedback people can train people to lower their blood pressure through mind control. Is it not possible to imagine that uncontrolled worry or extreme tension can contribute to cancer? Or, in the case of Cathy and many other patients like her, contribute to setting in motion an immunological defense against cancer?

Cathy and the Breast Biopsy

Cathy is really a composite of many not-so-favorite patients whose stories were related to me by a local gynecologist. She is the woman who receives an unfavorable biopsy. Breast biopsy or Pap smear, it matters not. Cathy goes into a tail spin. Cathy is certainly not the favorite patient either of her doctor, the hospital, the anesthesiologist, or the nurses. The moment that Cathy enters the hospital, she starts complaining. She begins threatening lawsuits. She mentions malpractice insurance, lawyers. She is hostile, aggressive, mean, downright nasty, and very often insulting. Cathy paces the hall the night before the operation. The nurses in vain give her all kinds of tranquilizing medicines and even morphine. To no avail. Cathy walks the hall. Cathy cries. Sometimes Cathy goes into religious hysteria. Cathy is up early the next morning, once again pacing the hall. When the doctor knows he has a patient like Cathy, he wants to get her on the table as soon as possible.

Cathy is not crazy, just a little bit hysterical. Her hysteria seems to pay off, because time after time that somewhat positive biopsy turns out to be nothing but a scare. Is this the link that the cancer researchers have been talking about? The woman who is self-controlled, mature, accepting, is willing to live with one left breast or accept a hysterectomy. She is the woman who does have cancer when the biopsy is uncertain. The Cathys of the world, who moan, groan, threaten lawsuits, and generally make themselves a large-scale nuisance, statistically, it can be shown, do not have cancer. Maybe there is a link between adrenalin, acute stress, increased respiration, and the whole hormonal system being thrown out of whack by stress. Perhaps hysteria and psychological denial mean that antibodies are set up that fight the cancer. The medical literature is very uncertain on this point. Nonetheless, there are data that do indicate that a person with this aberrant and semihysterical behavior oftentimes does not have cancer even when the biopsies are positive.

Excedrin Headache Number 92

The data for migraine headaches are as inconclusive as those for cancer in women. However, most medical researchers agree that migraine surely is psychosomatic and psychological. Certain characteristic traits are important in delineating the migraine patient. Some of these are
– obsessional, perfectionist character,
– high ambition and striving,
– inflexibility and conformity,
– anxiety and tension,
– difficulties dealing with and expressing hostility and aggression,
– self-driving and meticulousness.
More women than men suffer from migraines. Practically every migraine sufferer reports that after a period of emotional stress to which the patient reacts with suppressed rage and resentment, a migraine attack follows.

So migraine sufferers show obsessional traits and are hyperactive, tense, overt, anxious, and unable to express their hostility and tensions. What does all this mean in English? Well, perhaps the case of Milly and her headaches will help.

Milly and the Headaches

Milly is a forty-three-year-old working female who has no previous history of emotional instability. She reported her first attack of migraine during the time of stress. Changes in alcohol, diet, particularly cheeses and chocolate, hunger, loss of sleep, anger, frustration, work problems, personal problems—all contribute to Milly's migraine. The migraines occur at least twice a year and Milly has to take to her bed and often vomits.

Milly is a true obsessive-compulsive. That means she is a lint-picking perfectionist—the type of person who arranges her desk just so. The kind of woman who empties an ashtray the moment you put some ash in it. Indeed, Milly is a very nice person. She is usually always smiling. She never loses her temper. She never yells at her children. In short, Milly bottles up all her hostilities inside until bang! She suffers a migraine.

For one who has not suffered a migraine, they simply cannot be described. Nausea, an aura, or visual problems are often reported. Rooms sway. Beds heave up and down. The migraine sufferer reports throbbing headaches that last for several hours.

Sometimes drug therapy will help. But most of the time it simply will not. Migraines are a mystery. Migraines are psychosomatic. There may be a change in the weather that causes the migraine. It may be alcohol, cheese, or chocolate that triggers a migraine. No matter. We are still in the dark concerning the migraine sufferer.

As an addendum, I would like to report how Milly cured her headaches and pass this on to anyone who will send me twenty-five cents for this purely nonscientific information. Whenever Milly has a headache she immediately goes to the hairdresser, gets her hair done, and leans her head against the electric hairdryer; she claims that the vibration will immediately get rid of her attack. I suppose it works, but you have to feel well enough to get out of bed to go to the hairdresser. If that is the case, quite obviously the migraine is on the wane.

What Else Don't We Know?

Studies of migraine and cancer lead us down blind alleys. We are equally confused by other pieces of research dealing with physical stress, emotional stress, immunology, the central nervous system, and endocrine imbalance. Yet most medical researchers feel that there is a link between the psychological and the physical in relation to many illnesses.

Solomon reports on a series of studies that he and his colleagues made on rheumatoid arthritis patients. He writes that rheumatoid arthritics, compared to various control groups, were self-sacrificing, masochistic, conforming, self-conscious, shy, inhibited, and perfectionistic. Also, female arthritic patients were nervous, tense, worried, moody, depressed, concerned with the rejection they perceived from their mothers and the strictness they perceived from their fathers, and showed denial and inhibition of the expression of anger. Women with rheumatoid arthritis scored higher than healthy female family members on the MMPI scales reflecting inhibition of anger, anxiety, depression, compliance-subservience, conservatism, security-seeking, shyness, and introversion.

What is so interesting about the Solomon studies is that he compared three groups of female family members. One group were the rheumatoid arthritics. The second group were healthy or non-rheumatoid arthritics who had the rheumatoid factor in their blood. The third group were healthy (non-rheumatoid-arthritic) women without the rheumatoid factor in the sera. There is fairly good evidence that this rheumatoid factor contributes to rheumatoid arthritis or at least shows a predisposition to rheumatoid arthritis. The psychological tests showed that all three groups were highly anxious and low in self-esteem. The author concludes that to be physically healthy a person needs to be psychologically healthy. Solomon writes that the group *with* the rheumatoid factor in the sera (who should be predisposed to the disease) exhibited similar personality traits to those who actually had rheumatoid arthritis. However, Solomon claims that those women who didn't have rheumatoid arthritis adapted better. What is adaptation? If the personality types are similar, the adaptation mechanisms should be similar and the physical symptoms also. Once again, medical research can only provide intriguing leads.

All these studies dealing with rheumatoid arthritis never indicate whether the depressed, worried, harassed, rejected, masochistic woman behaved in this manner before the onset of rheumatoid arthritis or after. Similarly, research dealing with duodenal ulcers, emotionally related gastritis, and ulcerative colitis indicate that extreme and constant stress plays a contributing role in these stomach abnormalities. How much, however, is the moot point. Some people can stand stress much better than others. Let us look at some success stories.

Superprofessional Mom

Margaret is the kind of woman that everybody hates. She is happily married, and she has three well-adjusted children. Her house is clean. She is a well-respected professional in the field of advertising. She does not have a psychiatrist, but she does have a live-in maid. Margaret is a super mom of the first order. She's been known to put a roof on her garage over a weekend. At other times she will fly to Bermuda for a vacation, usually taking one or two of her children along. Her husband adores her. She dresses with good taste and jogs around the neighborhood nightly to keep her figure.

What makes Margaret run? Well, Margaret is one of those people who seem to thrive on stress. She enjoys her children. She enjoys her job, has plenty of hobbies, doesn't smoke, drinks only mildly, gets lots of fresh air and exercise. However, remember Margaret is in an upper-middle-class bracket, where a great deal of her tensions can be relieved by buying services. The full-time maid removes the strain of cooking and cleaning. The trips to Bermuda or Arizona paid for by Visa also provide a welcome relief from tension.

Margaret is an intelligent woman in her mid-forties who has seen her colleagues and peers felled by coronaries or maimed by ulcers. But Margaret's pattern of existence is contrary to what we usually talk about in relation to the type-A behavior pattern. Type A is the person who walks fast, eats fast, writes fast, does everything with haste, bottles up emotions, and is coronary prone. While this description may seem an analysis of Margaret's life style, it is really not. From grade school to high school and college, Margaret's life has always been active. In the eyes of the world, she is a success. And she is.

Margaret is truly one of the golden people. Happy, healthy children, devoted husband, promotions at work, and even professional accolades attest to the fact that whatever she is doing, she is doing it right. Perhaps her secret is that she has the sense to realize when stress is catching up with her. When stress and strain are too much for her, she escapes out of town with her husband, away from her children, away from her job, and enjoys a weekend on a secluded beach somewhere. Periodically she checks into one of the miracle spas and sleeps and diets and jogs. That's all very nice to do if you earn over fifty thousand dollars a year. Unfortunately, most of us can't do that. However, Margaret's life is an interesting example of the high need achiever in an important position who is not a psychiatric problem or an alcoholic or popping pills. Notwithstanding bad novels and afternoon soap operas, there really is no reason why all of us have to pay for our success in bleeding ulcers or divorces. Yet most of us don't have such marvelous success and have to find other means of support.

A Jewel Without Price

Ruby manages quite nicely without a full-time maid, without a husband, without very much money, but with a great deal of peer and religious support. Ruby is a widow with two teen-age sons. Ruby is also black and lives in a crime-ridden area. Ruby is the kind of woman that Margaret hires to look after Margaret's children. A hard-working woman who often holds down two and sometimes three menial, badly paying jobs, Ruby is another Type-A, coronary-prone personality.

Somehow she manages to survive in the face of crushing poverty and overwhelming odds that would defeat a lesser person. Ruby lives and survives for her children. She is firmly convinced that her boys will go to college and become successes. So far, they are doing fairly well and not hanging around the corner with many of their contemporaries. However, Ruby has centered her life on her boys and her church. She says that "it's hard enough being black without being Catholic—and I'm both." Her faith has provided comfort and solace, night after night, when she has been unable to sleep. Many a night, she has paced the floor with rosary in hand, praying for the strength to continue the night and face the next day. Priests have become father figures to the boys. The local parochial school gave both boys scholarships and the teachers take an active interest in the boys' schoolwork.

Ruby can barely read and write, but she is as success-oriented and college-conscious as any white, middle-class, suburban matron. She knows that the way to success in the

United States is through education. So far, so good. The boys are motivated and even inspired by her example. I talked to one of the children, who said, "I couldn't disappoint Momma. She lives every day for us. She works long hours so that we can have a decent place to live and go to school. She used to spank us terribly if we didn't do our homework. Now we know that the only thing that will please her is for us to go to a good school. I don't know what I want to do right now. All I know is that I have to *be* somebody. There are all sorts of things that I have to do. I have to justify her faith in me."

Ruby knows that her peace of mind comes to her only through her religion. Every day, she steals time early in the morning for early mass. Without the mass, her life is devoid of meaning. Loneliness, mounting bills, worries over the future, worries over everything—prayer helps. And apparently it does. Ruby is well adjusted, even though she would have good reason to be a little neurotic or maybe even a lot upset. Her health is good and she knows how important that can be. She prays daily for the courage to continue to work and for health to enable her to work. She worries and prays over the boys. She is well aware that one of the worst things that could happen to her or her boys would be a serious illness or operation that would mean losing all her savings. Does that mean that the power of prayer staves off a hysterectomy? Maybe yes, maybe no. The mind-body link via prayer and belief is as old as the biblical admonition to "take up thy bed and walk." Lourdes, miracle cures, miracles. At least it helps Ruby. Prayer never helped my friend Kate.

Kate and the Ménage à Trois

My friend Kate used to be a walking catalogue of psychosomatic symptoms. She had skin problems, colitis, diverticulitis, and insomnia, and her hands shook a lot.

When I last saw Kate, she looked marvelous. She hadn't looked so well in years. Her skin was glowing and her eyes were twinkling. She and I had grown apart after our respective marriages. Kate went with her prestigious husband to a prestigious West Coast university and they fell into every fad and fancy that Californians embraced in the sixties and the seventies. Kate's husband became a fashionable Marxist commentator. So fashionable and chic that it cost $1,500 for George to appear on a panel to denigrate the conference organizers and predicate the imminent demise of capitalism. Then George and Kate spent the money. They went to Esalen for group "awareness." They went into transactional analysis. Nude swimming and vegetarianism were just part of the package.

Of course, George had his affairs and Kate had an occasional weekend away, but they maintained some semblance of propriety for the children's sake. However, George got enthusiastic about the idea of Open Marriage and Self-Expression. He persuaded Kate that three was not only company but that a *ménage-à-trois* with one of George's graduate students would be liberating. Only, Kate didn't agree. Kate told me about how she finally woke up from her nightmare:

> George used to bring Myra [the girlfriend] home after
> class and they would go upstairs to make love while I

stayed in the kitchen and cooked dinner. We would all have a civilized dinner—Myra, George, the kids, and me. I would dutifully clean up. Myra would go home. The kids would do their homework and George would work on his papers. I thought it was all pretty crazy, especially since I was getting no sex at all, because George was burnt out with Myra.

So, one day, I was stirring the spaghetti sauce and trying to convince myself that I was liberated, sexually aware, not a castrating wife, and one of the harbingers of a new life style. I stirred the spaghetti sauce and got madder and madder. I thought of how shocked my mother would be. How shocked George's mother would be. How angry I would be if anyone knew that we were carrying on like this with the children in the house. I stirred the spaghetti sauce faster and faster. Then I thought, this is MY house, this is MY kitchen, that is MY bed, and God damn it all to Hell, that is MY husband.

So I went upstairs with the big cooking spoon still in my hand and burst into the bedroom. I saw the two of them on the bed and I was so angry I really could have killed them. I started banging both of them with the cooking ladle and screaming at both of them to get the hell out of MY house and to never come back again.

Like the dog chasing its tail, mental stress produces physical and psychological reactions, which trigger more stress. The woman who worries and frets about her husband's infidelity gets a serious skin rash; she can't sleep because of the itching rash, and she now worries over the mounting doctor bills. She and her husband can't have sex, because her skin is so tender. Her husband continues and even increases his sordid little affairs. And the pattern continues on and on.

Many women are simply unable to reach a level of insight into their problems and lay out a series of alternate solutions. The clue to mental and physical health is this kind of insight.

Self-Appraisal

The healthy personality or the informed woman can analyze herself. She can recognize the warning signals of stress: overweight, shortness of breath, insomnia, pains in the neck, arm, or chest, drinking too much, excessive cigarette smoking, menstrual problems, crying jags, or fits of depression. The list can be extended to every shortcoming known to man or woman. The important thing is to deal with the stress in an intelligent fashion. But, most of the time, we are neither informed nor brilliant. Like the fish that never knows that it swims in water, we are often so enmeshed in personal problems and multiple roles that we cannot see how the demands of society, family, job, and self can be met.

However, your body will start giving you the necessary signals. That's why it pays to be on good terms with your family physician, gynecologist, ophthalmologist, and above all dentist. Just like your GP, your family dentist will be the first to notice signs of extreme stress. People under stress are very likely to grind their teeth. Tooth-grinding can occur during a meeting, where only a slight twitch in the cheek shows, or while you're asleep during the night. Broken fillings and fractured teeth indicate suppressed anger. As a champion tooth-grinder myself, I am living testimony to the relationship between stress and high dental bills. Usually my dentist will peer into my mouth, hem and haw a little, and then ask, "Whom do you want to bite today?" Dental researchers report that tooth-grinding is one of the most serious dental problems in the United States today.

Yet we not so merrily grind our teeth through life while collecting a few ulcers and coronaries on the way. We seem to be completely oblivious to those important stress signals our body sends to us.

Make a Health List, Not a Laundry List

We've seen that there is a relationship between stress and disease—whether it be broken teeth, ulcers, or migraine headaches. Even though psychiatrists will tell you that only neurotics make lists, perhaps you ought to make a health list, not a laundry list. On one side of the page, write down current physical symptoms. In the middle of the page, write down the date when you think these symptoms first appeared. Then, on the far-right side of the page, try to link that date with some important stressful event in your life. Remember, stressful occasions may be happy ones, like marriage, graduation, promotion, new job, just as well as those unhappy moments, such as death, divorce, or moving. You will probably surprise yourself with how interrelated life-stress events and diseases may be. Maybe you want to think over the past winter. How many times did you have a cold? When did it occur? Did you have the flu? Once? Twice? An even-steven bet is that you had the flu or a bad cold around Christmas time. Why is it that you always end up having a head cold on New Year's Eve? Do you always go out on New Year's Eve? Do you hate going out on New Year's?

There is cyclical variation to illness. Biofeedback researchers and scientists interested in the phenomena of death report that death rates increase immediately after important occasions such as Christmas, New Year's, Easter, the Fourth of July. Seriously ill patients can stave off death until important events have passed. Terminally ill patients will die *after* their birthday, *after* the wedding anniversary, *after* the son or grandson has graduated from college, or *after* a long-awaited party has taken place. Patients can will themselves to live until a long-awaited occasion has finally taken place.

The cyclical variation in death rates makes perfect sense if you give credence to the mind-body link. People can will themselves to die—or they can stave off death for a few days or a few months. While these variations seem somewhat grand opera-ish, nevertheless people do die at different rates and almost invariably *after* important national or religious holidays or special family occasions. Once more, researchers are turning to the exotic Eastern religions and anthropological reports for clues to the biochemical/biological feedback mechanisms.

This kind of research is not new; Walter Cannon wrote extensively on voodoo death in the mid nineteen thirties. Cannon tried to understand why people who had been hexed, died. Simply died. A little curse and they just died. Cannon analyzed the reports of voodoo death and came to the conclusion that the person who was hexed, believed in and had faith in the power of the hex; the person was frightened and the body reacted. Shock killed the person. Voodoo hex produced fright; fright triggered an anxiety response; shock resulted; and death ensued. An interesting equation. Very few persons paid attention to Cannon's writings, until Selye began to focus on the concept of stress and general adaptation syndromes.

While we do know a great deal about the detrimental effects of stress, we are still in the dark ages regarding the euphoric effects of "eustress." There are some people who literally thrive on stress. Without constant excitement, they would curl up their toes and probably die.

We don't know the effects of such adapting mechanisms as Yoga, Transcendental Meditation, Zen, religious ecstasy. Medical researchers are now investigating phenomena that used to be dismissed as mumbo jumbo. Maybe we had better return to Greek philosophy and seek once more the same kind of mind-body that Hippocrates advocated.

Back to the Greeks

List making has a purpose. Socrates told us, Know thyself. Follow his advice and learn to know your insides and your outsides. What kind of physical condition you are in relates to what kind of state your body is in, what kinds of food you eat, what kinds of cosmetics you use. Make up some more lists. What kinds of things do you like doing? In another list, what kinds of things do you dislike doing? Do you cope easily with stress? Do you cope intellectually with stress or have physical reactions? You don't need a therapist to help you make up those lists. Maybe you should start them one night and even set them aside for a week. What is unique about your life? about the many roles that you play? What contributes to your physical and mental healthiness or unhealthiness? Your physical condition directly correlates with your mental state.

Illness as a Club

Most importantly, you should analyze how you feel when you are ill. Do you enjoy your illness? Illness can be used as a club over those whom you love or whom you hate. Probably your reaction to the preceding statement is "Nonsense." No. Not nonsense. We all know cases of aged parents who control their children via their illness. What housewife with a "bad back" has not kept her husband in thrall? Secretaries control their bosses with gory menstrual-problem stories. Victorian literature is filled with tales of fainting wives and cranky, aging parents.

Illness works very well, because we're all taught the precepts of fair play. One of the rules of fair play involves fighting equal against equal. Someone who has a heart condition or ulcers or menstrual problems is not fair game. The cry in this relationship is "I'm sick. So be nice to me!" That's why parents are at a decided disadvantage with a bed-wetting or a stuttering child. The child who stutters says, "But I can't help it." The child who wets the bed cries out, "But I was asleep."

Nonsense once again. A good therapist tries to find out why the child is so hostile toward the parent. What annoys the parent most of all: stuttering? bed wetting? The child subconsciously vows to pay the parent back for real or imagined grievances. The kid stammers. Or wets the bed. The parent is furious. The parent can't blame the child for something he/she is unable to control. The illness club bangs the parent right over the head.

And that of course relates to the question "How do you feel when you are sick?" Another question that should be asked, in tandem, is "When do you get sick?" Do you get sick when there is an important deadline at work? Do you get sick and does your back give out just before your husband leaves on a business trip without you? When you are sick, does your family wait on you hand and foot? Are you the center of attention? Do you get driven to and from doctors' appointments and hospitals? If the answer to these questions is "Yes" and if you have more than one serious illness a year or more than one operation per year, your problem is probably not in your body but in your head. Since it is markedly unfair on the battlefield of family fights for a person to pick on a "sick" member, then the person who is sick—mentally or physically—has already won the battle.

It is too extreme to state that all illness is psychosomatic. Nonetheless, most illness has a psychological cause. Illness may be a luxury, a luxury in the sense of psychological benefit for the person who is ill. But if you can will yourself to be sick, maybe psychological insights will help you to will yourself well. It requires some severe and painful self-analysis. Who are you? What are your roles? What good does your illness accomplish for you?

6

Stress, Marriage, and Children

SOCIOLOGIST Jessie Bernard has shown that marriage is much more beneficial to husbands than to wives. Marriage is a stress-reducing mechanism for men and a stress-*producing* one for women. What every working woman knows is that marriage produces extra work. Two cannot live as cheaply as one, but one usually ends up doing the work for two. Most men cannot cope with the single, widowed, or divorced life, but women can. The traditional sex-role division of labor is always at work. Women do the cooking, shopping, washing, sock-sorting, and all the associated Mickey Mouse housework, while the husband pounds nails or watches the football game.

Every Woman Needs a Wife

A few seasons back, there was a very bad TV program about a working woman who could not cope with the demands of house and job. She and her husband contracted to have a servant; but the catch was that the servant was really a wife. The sexy-sexist overtones of this *ménage à trois* contributed to the demise of the program. Nonetheless, every working woman needs a wife. In fact, when Texan Ann Armstrong was appointed by Lyndon Johnson to be ambassador to London, the Department of State hired a woman to act in the role of the "ambassador's wife." No one expected Ann Armstrong's Texas millionaire husband to behave in the nurturant, female-entertainer, adjunct-wife role. And so a young woman was paid ten thousand dollars a year to arrange flowers, make seating arrangements, organize the foreign-service-officer wives, and in general fulfill those functions that ambassadors' wives throughout the world have done on an unpaid basis. No wonder, then, that in the mid 1970s the foreign-service-officer wives engaged in a small revolt. Women's liberation and a burgeoning sense of self contributed to the fso wives' pertinent and timely demands. These women said that they refused to act as unpaid help to the lady ambassador. So now foreign-service-officer wives do not have to dance attendance upon the ambassador's wife or engage in charity-balls or the time-consuming tea-party chitchat that forms the very basis of the foreign-service-officer wife's day. Similarly, officers' wives' clubs, whether air force, army, or navy, are slowly dying of atrophy. Officers' wives and even generals' wives are getting advanced degrees, teaching school, finding jobs, or simply staying home and reading rather than being lady bountiful at the officers' club.

Being a wife-mother is burden enough. Particularly in the United States, where competency usually means upward mobility and achievement. The wife-mother in the United States is expected to fulfill a multitude of roles that in other parts of the world are fulfilled by other women: servant, laundress, cook, gardener, seamstress, baby sitter, storyteller, protocol officer, geisha girl, mistress, wit, juggler, performer, confidante, psychologist-therapist, and so on. Periodically, insurance salesmen like to put ads in women's magazines, trying to entice wives to encourage their husbands to buy life insurance policies on the wives. At a very minimum base salary, ten thousand dollars a year in dribs and drabs would go out in salaries to fulfill these various roles—excluding probably the geisha and mistress roles. There are of course myriad tasks that many women fulfill, such as den mother, soccer coach, occasional photographer, and the general molder of the next generation. While there is a Parkinson's law of housework, the wife-mother role is never finished. Moreover, it is essentially boring. There is just so much fulfillment in picking up towels off the bathroom floor and washing dirty socks. This is not meant to denigrate the wife-mother role but only to point out that the glorification of housework that took place in the 1950s thanks to Phyllis McGinley's poetry and some very bad TV shows really is an exaggeration.

However, more is expected of women. And less is realized. Typically American, we demand more and more of our young women in this wife-mother role than any one person can fulfill. Madison Avenue hype contributes to this constant feeling of inadequacy. Yellow wax on the kitchen floor means you are a very bad person. Your son fails grade-two mathematics and you fail as a mother. Really, cleanliness is not next to godliness, but godliness is equal to cleanliness. That cleanliness is achieved by buying and using magic products.

Myth of Labor-saving Devices

One of the greatest myths sold to the American woman is that the greater the number of labor-saving appliances in the home the greater the amount of labor that is saved. This is false. Home economists write that the more machines that come into the home the more time is required to use them. The kinds of tasks that our grandmother put off from one week to one month now are expected to be immediate, constant features of our lives. As a child, I can remember, we washed clothes only once a week. Monday, indeed, was laundry day. Some of our clothes were grimy, some of them were tattle-tale gray, and most of my father's shirts had a ring around the collar. But that was the best that mother could do and we all put up with it. Now we are expected to have clean clothes constantly. You use your towel only once, you wear a blouse only once, you change the sheets and, God forbid, even iron them. Obviously, if you own a sewing machine you are expected to sew. Magic irons mean more ironing. Washers, dryers, vacuum cleaners—you name it and it means more work.

Even now with working women the magic time savers are Faustian pacts with the electric company. Crock-pots, microwave ovens, electric crepe makers, electric can openers, and the ultimate in laziness, the electric vegetable peeler, all add to our time in the kitchen rather than lessen the moments spent there. But that's all right. These appliances help alleviate the guilt of not spending eight to ten hours in the kitchen preparing gourmet meals. Our mothers, the cookbook, the Sunday supplement, and even nutritionists tell us we should prepare beautiful, well-arranged, nutritional, exciting meals for our family, friends, lovers, and even the family dog. Since working women do not have the time to do that, they suffer from acute guilt pangs that are alleviated by buying and even using these electrical gadgets. Of course, the Sunday supplements will tell us that the new working wife also has her gourmet cook husband helping her in the kitchen. T'aint so. As a matter of fact, t'aint so even in the best of communal societies.

Worms in Elysium

The 1960s saw a flight from middle-class mores into the good life—out into the country, communing with everybody. Fleeing from supposedly bourgeois capitalist oppression, men and women sought new ways of expressing themselves under this open, blue sky. Not only were the women handed around from man to man but they escaped from middle-class oppression to a new and very often more vicious kind of sexual oppression. Traditional male-female roles were found rampant in Utopia. While there might not have been too much laundry done, the cooking still remained. Women went to the kitchen and stayed.

Similarly, even in utopian societies such as the Israeli kibbutz, there was a flight *from* equality to sexual oppression. Rae Lesser Blumberg wrote an interesting paper in 1974 on the flight from the tractor to the kitchen. Her analyses have been borne out by Israeli women social scientists who have shown how Israeli women were slowly but surely pushed out of tasks ranging from driving tractors and administering the kibbutzim to the low-level tasks of laundry, kitchen, and nursery. There was a push-pull effect. Oriental Jews poured into Israel in the 1950s and had to be quickly socialized and then absorbed into the population. The two places where this was accomplished were the Army and the kibbutzim. The more men that there are available for given tasks the more likely the men will be assigned to leadership (and "male") positions. And there is a rank hierarchy of tasks. Driving tractors is "fun" and "masculine," while cooking for two hundred people is "drudgery" and also—by fiat—"feminine." Also associated with the flight from equality to a reaffirmation of traditional-sex-role jobs was a pronatalist Israeli governmental policy. Thus the most important thing that a woman could do was to have children. Pregnancy limited the time and effort that women could expend on outdoor work. But I could never understand why pregnancy limited Israeli women's administrative ability. However, Israeli women did abdicate leadership roles in the kibbutzim.

Nonetheless, the 1960s communal societies in the Southwest, combined with the utopian failure of the Kibbutz, show us that when people seek a perfect society, the perfection is undoubtedly and always male. The ultimate question of course is, Who does the laundry and the cooking,

the cleaning and the dusting? As the women's liberationists
are fond of pointing out, "Housework is politics."

Housework Politics

It is tragic that the kibbutzim and the new life style
would founder on the issue of housewifery. But it happened. And it still does happen. Many of the more liberated couples that I know, while living together, had to work
out their housewife chores together. Something strange
happened the moment they made their illegal liaison legal.
That something was housework. We do know there is a
Parkinson's law of housewifery. That is, the more time that
one has to fulfill a task, the greater amount of time that
task will take. So if you have all day long to wash the floors,
make the beds, and dry the dishes—it will take all day to do
these chores. However, when the husband and wife or male
and female members of a "relationship" both work, the
tasks, according to the ideology, ought to be and must be
shared. So much for ideology.

Beautiful relationships that begin with guitars, music,
gardenia-scented air, and the crashing of waves upon the
beach founder miserably over who is to sort the socks. It's
nice to think that most males do not have their masculinity
wrapped up in carrying out the garbage. Still, male children avoid female jobs. Cooking is fun once in a while.
The young husband can afford to whip up a magnificent
Caesar salad with a superb dressing and choose a $3.99
wine—once in a while and on Saturdays. But it's awfully
boring to get off the subway every night and start slinging

hash. He makes the gourmet meal. She cooks the hamburgers. That's what happened with Georgie.

Georgie and the Marriage Contract

The story of Georgie is not unlike that of many women in their late twenties or thirties. Brought up by a puritan upper-middle-class-intellectual mother, Georgie wholeheartedly believed in equality, women's liberation, and equal pay for equal work, and really wasn't that anxious to get married. Like the Jacqueline who became a Jackie, our heroine is a Georgina who became a Georgie. With her masculine-feminine name she also had masculine-feminine values. Georgie had had several long-term relationships that usually ended because, as she explains it, "Housework is a critical issue." Finally she took up with a man she firmly considered to have all the virtues of the liberated male. They kept two apartments and periodically lived with each other for over a year. It was moonlight and roses with occasional spats, but things went along quite nicely. Besides, she would withdraw from the relationship when she needed to do her laundry, and he never brought his dirty things over to her apartment. They finally decided to legalize their irregular union, not for tax purposes but mainly to make both families feel better. Marriage changed everything.

The moment that Georgie and her lover married, he refused to share chores with her. No more clearing off the table or doing the dishes. He would prepare meals every once in a while, but his solution to Georgie's having had a bad day was to go out for a greasy-spoon meal anywhere, so that *Georgie* didn't have to cook. The more she explained the more adamant he became. The fights got worse. The sex tapered off. And now they have separated. Fortunately, it happened before they started a family. Problems are bad enough being the working wife. Being the working wife-mother is even worse.

How to Survive Being a Working Mother

In the 1940s and '50s, Philip Wylie railed against the whole group of women in his book *Generation of Vipers*. Wylie invented the term "momism" for the mother who devours her young, the mother who instills guilt in her children—primarily the male—for all the sacrifices she has made for them. Nowadays women are supposed to fulfill themselves outside the home and thus avoid instilling guilt in the future generation. However, most of the time, the working mother gets an "F" in mothering over her non-working neighbor mothers. Interestingly enough, Nye and Hoffman showed that women who work and hate their jobs have less guilt and better-adjusted children than women who like their jobs. One rather startling finding indicates that women can alleviate the guilt of leaving their children alone if they must work because of financial reasons, divorce, abandonment, widowhood, or whatever. However, the mother who is in comfortable enough circumstances and receives joy from her job correspondingly increases her guilt level. Many of my working-mother acquaintances commiserate with each other over fulfilling middle-class expectations of what a mother ought to be in combination with demands of a profession. Men seem to be able to separate job and home roles much easier than women. We are still stuck with traditional sex-role concepts.

What happens when both parents work, all children are school age, and one of them is running a temperature of 104°? Which parent stays home? There seems to be no way other than tossing a coin. Most, if not all, of the time, the mother performs the nurturing, nursing role, not the father. Several working professional wife-mother friends of mine and I have come up with a list of do's and don'ts to alleviate this particular stress. Some work and some do not. First and foremost, the working parent must remember that guilt is a non-affordable luxury. Guilt is a very nice game that is played by non-working parents against working parents, in-laws against their daughters-in-law, children against their parents, and probably worst of all, schoolteachers against parents. But no single life style reaches nirvana. That is, non-working mothers do not necessarily form a generation of vipers and a working mother does not guarantee a juvenile delinquent. Overcoming guilt is not easy. As a matter of fact, guilt can be an excuse for all the things you do and that you don't do. Once a mother has sorted out the reasons for working—money, fame, self-fulfillment, psychological need—then she can't play a guilt game. The mother who works because she has to is less likely to feel guilty. But a reasonably comfortable, middle-class, well-educated woman who works because she wants to is caught on the horns of a dilemma. Well, she doesn't have to be there and she can unimpale herself from those horns by simply not engaging in stressful introspection of this sort.

Again, however, a whole series of adjustments are necessary.

Obviously, for the working mother the most important thing is to insure that the children have adequate supervision of some sort. For non-school-age children the difficulty is equally stressful. Nonetheless, mothers can investigate the possibilities of day-care centers with varying hours, the possibility of an in-law's coming to stay, after-school teenage baby sitters, senior citizens as baby sitters, and of course the ultimate: the live-in maid. While live-in help at first glance seems to be completely out of the realm of possibility for most women, it can indeed work out. Several friends of mine have made arrangements with local community hospitals or nursing schools and theology seminaries for live-in students to perform household chores, make meals, and be there when the children leave and come home from school. A word of warning probably is necessary at this stage: avoid at all costs graduate students. Juniors and seniors will work out, but graduate students have invariably, for myself and my friends, proven to be absolute disasters. The graduate student, whether male or female, is wrapped up in the master's thesis or the Ph.D. dissertation. With the attendant stresses that they bring into the home, they cannot fulfill their obligations to you or to your children. Of course there are attendant difficulties with some of these other solutions, such as having an in-law coming to stay forever. This may be somewhat of a strain on your marital relationships or your own personal psyche. Sometimes a mother-in-law baby sitter simply just isn't worth it. Unfortunately, day-care centers do not usually have variable hours and you find the working mother rushing across town in commuter traffic trying desperately to pick up a child before the center closes. Industry, government, and business, however, are adopting "flexitime," varying hours that help the working mother and in turn reduce absenteeism on the job. More and more women work. As more women who work are mothers with young children, society will continue to make realistic adaptations for the care of these children.

The major adaptation, however, once again still has to be in the mind of the mother. She cannot be all things to her children. There is no possible way she can be the sooper-dooper mom, getting an "A" every single day for her mothering. The house will not be as clean, the meals will probably not be as nutritious, and the children probably not quite as happy as they might be. The children will demand time and the mother must learn to adapt to their demands. Working mothers interact intensively with their children in the little time they do have. Thus, once a woman recognizes her own demands, her own needs, and those of her children, she can start to alleviate some of the stress of the role of working mother and wife. Otherwise poor Mom gets blamed for everything. Let us look at why men as single parents don't feel guilty.

Single-parent Dad Versus Single-parent Mom

Some of the saddest statistics in the United States are those concerned with divorce. One out of every three marriages end in divorce, except in some northeastern areas of the United States, and in California, large midwestern cities such as Chicago, where one out of every two marriages flounder. There are areas in San Francisco and Los Angeles where seven out of ten or eight out of ten marriages in the upper-middle-class suburban areas are second tries. Traditionally, in a divorce case the woman gets custody of the children. The father pays child support until such time as the woman remarries. At least that *was* the traditional way of dividing up responsibilities and priorities. Now there is a new phenomenon: the single-parent *father*. As women themselves and the mass media began to wrestle with the question of traditional sex roles and the "natural" idea of a maternal role, so judges began to realize that fathers often made better parents than drunken or amoral mothers. At the same time, men began to accept the nurturant, loving parent role—and they demanded their children. Of course, single-parent fathers as a result of death of spouse have occurred long before this. There were rare occasions when a father would be granted custody of the children in a particularly brutal situation. But if we examine the difference between single-parent male and single-parent female, maybe we can see some stress-alleviating situations that women can use.

Remember, though, that widowers or divorced fathers are congratulated for the superhuman job that they are performing as parent and employee, whereas divorced mothers do not receive the same kind of praise. That is unfortunate.

However, men usually seem to be able to cope on an inestimably higher level of efficiency than women. Perhaps dirt, clutter, and mess do not reflect upon the male single parent's ability as much as they do upon women. One very good friend of mine has developed a series of unique methods of coping with his three growing sons.

George goes downtown every once in a while and buys himself and his sons four dozen purple socks. When I asked George why the color purple rather than anything else, he replied jovially, "Purple socks are always on sale." Since George and his three sons are all pretty much the same size, all the socks can be washed at the same time and divided up among the four males. When a sock has a hole in it, it is thrown out. Since all socks are the same color, there is no necessity to wrap them up in neat matching sets and put them carefully into a drawer. Each one has a sock drawer composed of nothing but purple socks. George also explains that they can get dressed in the dark very easily because they don't have to worry about matching their socks. As a side effect, the underwear is tinged a pale violet. It doesn't really matter to George or to his boys. Each boy has the responsibility for one third of the house, and George went out and bought three vacuum cleaners. The vacuum-cleaner owner is royally chewed out and his allowance held out if his third of the house is found to be messy or untidy. George contends that never before has he realized that mess and clutter on the part of his children is a political act of hostility against him. Sometimes George's single-parent role is too much and he threatens to become a runaway parent. He so far has maintained his status and remained at home. Superb organization, freezers, huge cooking batches, cooking ahead, microwave ovens, crockpots, any possible method that will help him in maintaining his sanity, George will buy. Of course his life is further simplified by the fact that he has three adolescents who can care for themselves. And because of their mother's long, lingering death, the boys and their father are extremely close, loving, and care for each other dearly.

While George is managing very well, the age of the children is a stress-reducing or stress-producing factor: George (or a single-parent mother) suffers less stress if the children can feed, clothe, and take care of themselves. The younger the children the greater the amount of care and feeding and thus the greater the stress for the mother (or father). Also, the income level of women is usually much less than men of comparable education. If a woman cannot hire adequate help or there is no day-care center in her neighborhood or she has no relatives to help drive the children to dentist and doctor appointments or she has a demanding job with long hours, then high levels of stress will occur.

Also, there is a difference in male-female standards of cleanliness. While I have known many a dirty female housekeeper and many a spotless male bachelor, most women seem to have higher standards than most men. From early childhood, women are taught that dirt is evil, while boys are told that it's OK to get dirty and make a mess. Girls learn very soon that kitchens must be spotless and meals unique. Most men feel that as long as the kitchen is reasonably tidy and there is some food on the table, life will continue. There is one existential question that most working mothers must ask themselves: "Can you use paper plates?" If the answer is yes, you have overcome your guilt trip. Think of how many times you would get out of quarrels as to who would do the dishes simply by using paper plates.

Divorce, Death, Separation, and Stress

In the Holmes and Rahe scale of traumatic events, death of a spouse and divorce top the list. Divorce and death both produce depression. Depression, on the other hand, may produce divorce.

The loss of a spouse, whether through divorce, death, or separation, produces anxiety symptoms manifested in diverticulitis, gastritis, colitis, depression, loneliness, and even suicide. Divorce or death of a spouse produces bereavement symptoms. Researchers report that loss of spouse may result in increased alcoholic intake, increased use of drugs or tranquilizers, insomnia, tears, hyperventilation, malaise, or agitation.

Anybody who tells you that she is withstanding her divorce well or that she has gotten over the death of a spouse . . . is exaggerating. My sister-in-law had a head-on collision returning home after her final divorce decree was granted. Another friend of mine nearly sliced her finger off the night that her husband left her for another woman. Again, you don't have to be more than an amateur therapist to realize that forgetting, anxiety reactions, agitated depression, or simply going to bed for a couple of days are the result of this grieving process. For those contemplating divorce and those trying to find their way out of the grieving process, a support system is an absolute necessity. Unfortunately, in this migratory society in which we live, we are forced to seek a support system at the very precise moment when we are unable to do anything on our own. Parents Without Partners is an organization well equipped to help the widow or the divorcee. It usually is an *ad hoc* or after-the-fact kind of operation. That is, people usually seek out Parents Without Partners when they come to the realization that they need a support system; they are on their way back to mental healthiness. Nonetheless, if a close friend or relative is going through a grieving/ bereavement process as the result of death or divorce, urge him very strongly to find Parents Without Partners. Getting together, the occasional dating, and the picnics and outings are organized with the realization that there are lots of other people who are not married and life can go on in the single and unblissful stage. It helps close open wounds.

Being in a not-married status, individuals are extremely prone to physical and mental illnesses. Divorce and death trauma guarantee some kind of a stomach upset, maybe pneumonia, extremely bad colds, or, if nothing else, a few crying jags. It is difficult to be the friend of a widow or a recent divorcee, because they are usually so terribly boring. They tell you the same story over and over and over again:

"Oh, how I wish I had been a better wife."

"I wish we had taken that trip we had planned."

"I would have done things so differently if I had had the chance." The names, the dates, the places may change, but the litany is always the same: Given a second chance, we know how much better things would be.

Men and women who suffer from separation anxiety— death or divorce—usually turn their hostility inward. Traditionally, rituals involve weeping, wailing, rending of garments, and tearing of hair and gnashing of teeth. Some societies insure there will be a great din associated with the funeral: professional mourners are hired to make lots of noise and bewail the dear departed. In our society, where the dear departed is a spouse via law court or a husband courtesy of a coronary, we're expected to behave properly. Only a few little discreet tears are allowed, and widows cover their faces with veils. Divorcees are expected to raise a gallant cup of champagne. The singular lack of emotionality undoubtedly contributes to our stomach problems and rampant depression.

Probably the best thing to do with the divorce or death bereavement period is to recognize the various kinds of problems that we will encounter. Also, you have to set a limit as to how long this grieving period will last. The general rule of thumb seems to be from six to twelve weeks. Of course, death in our society is more traumatic than divorce. Therefore you are allowed a longer mourning period for the loss of a spouse, rather than a divorce. Friends and relatives will usually marshall their forces and support you beautifully for a week or ten days, or sometimes up to three weeks, depending upon the age of the person involved. But they usually then demand a stiff upper lip and a re-entry into society. That's not as easy as it looks.

The Not-so-merry Divorcee

After many years in a loveless marriage and in a psychologically brutalizing relationship, Janet sued for and easily obtained a divorce. Janet was convinced that she could return to teaching and was dismayed to find an oversupply of teachers. She obtained a reasonably well-paying administrative job in a local community college but had to fend for herself. The woman-alone syndrome hit with a vengeance, along with a devastating snow storm. Janet was expected to turn up at her job even though her children's school was canceled. She had to dig herself out of the driveway several times, lug groceries up and down icy walks, and cope with frozen pipes. All this was combined with adolescent rebellion and erratic alimony and child support.

Janet looked forward to her post-divorce freedom as a time when she could engage in "self-actualization" and "fulfilling herself as a person" sexually, intellectually, psychologically, and individually. At least that's what *Cosmopolitan* magazine told her was going to happen. Janet, like so many divorcees and widows, found that she was rejected by her women friends because she was now a sexual threat to their home and harmony. Friends took sides (some with husband, some with her), but in the long run Janet didn't get invited to dinner parties. Janet discovered that, even though her husband had been emotionally detached from the marriage, at least he was there sometimes to cope with her two willful daughters. As for glamorous dates and wild sexual acrobatics, they still remained figments of her imagination.

Occasionally, Janet was asked out to dinner but *only* occasionally. She found that a woman in her very late thirties, pushing forty, was a non-salable commodity on the marriage/dating market. Her worries over supervising her children the nights that she did go out overshadowed any enjoyment that she might achieve on the date. Besides, she did not know how to act on a date. She had been married to the same man for so long that she had forgotten all the coquettish, flirting tricks necessary to salve a male ego. Even if she had had this bag of tricks at her disposal, it probably would have been to no avail. The men just weren't there. Janet had read in the advice columns all the things to do to meet men, but she had neither the time nor the physical energy to take sky-diving courses or improve her mind. She had to fix the plumbing, take the car to the garage, buy the groceries, and somehow ensure that her daughters would grow up to be responsible young women.

Finally Janet came to the realization that for several years—at least until the girls were in college—her life would be routine and monotonous. Once she adjusted to the fact that her fantasies would not be realized, her life became better. Janet finally had to have not only heart-to-heart talks but some enraged screaming matches with her daughters to ensure their co-operation. The girls were old enough to realize the burden that their mother was carrying. With occasional spats, they survived.

In part, Janet had been causing her own problems. In her desperate search for excitement and glamour, her fantasies outweighed the mundane details of living. In Janet's attempt to protect her daughters from the psychological tensions of a divorce, Janet had placed too much burden upon herself and had refused to trust the girls. Her life now circulates around a few friends at work, church, the girls' school activities, and an occasional trip out of town in their beat-up station wagon. It isn't very good and hardly very merry. But the three of them have adjusted and life goes on. Hers could hardly be called a success story, but at least it isn't a failure. Other stories don't work out so well.

Sally the Runaway Mother

Private detectives report now that their business largely comprises finding the runaway wife or the runaway mother. Traditional sex roles are being overthrown every day. Rather than frantic wives trying desperately to find a husband who has cut out on them, the roles have been reversed as women pack up and move out. Many women seem to realize that the gay divorcee's life is hardly fun and games. If indeed there is equality associated with the new ideology, then the woman has an equal right to walk out and dump the kids on her unsuspecting husband. The ratios seem to vary and there are no adequate statistics as to what the proportion of runaway wives is to runaway husbands. Nevertheless, the number of women who are walking out on husbands and children mounts daily.

Sally used to muse on a new life. Her new life never included her three school-age children, ages seven, nine, and eleven. Sally knew that if she was to have champagne and bubbles in the bathtub in a high-rise penthouse, three children were equal to three millstones.

Accordingly, one day she packed her bags, wrote a long, involved note to her husband, and moved out. Even Sally was not prepared for the storm of anger and vilification that broke about her head. Her own relatives, her in-laws, friends, neighbors, casual acquaintances, and the check-out boy at the supermarket rallied around her husband's cause. Sally really isn't or wasn't any worse than any man who became a runaway husband. Nonetheless, for a woman to abnegate the mother role is a fairly recent phenomenon in our sexual history. Whatever motherhood does mean, it's one way of differentiating between male and female. Men can become ex-fathers, but it's rare that a woman can become an ex-mother. Women are expected to behave in mothering ways.

At the very least, mothers are expected to care for their children. Only a wretched woman indeed would cast aside her very own flesh and blood. Sally did just that. And she did it quickly, surgically, without a qualm, and even with some perverse delight. Sally thought she was paying her husband back in kind for the nights that she had gotten up for the two-o'clock feeding, toilet training, manners at the table, and helping with the homework. She told herself that her husband had spent *his* time building *his* career while she and the children were left out of his plan of action.

Sally was bright enough to get a good job, she found a small apartment, and she learned to tolerate subways, slush, TV dinners, and evenings filled with Johnny Carson and Merv Griffin. Her fantasies never became realities. Through court orders, Sally was completely cut out of the children's lives. There is no real future reconciliation in store for Sally or her children. When Sally walked out it was for good.

Unfortunately, most women have such low-level, badly paid jobs that they are unable to find fulfillment in the workplace if their marital status or sex life is in complete chaos. Nonetheless, as more and more women enter middle management and rise to the executive board room, we will see the new phenomenon of the female workaholic supplanting that of the male workaholic. Is this a better symbol? I think not.

7

Stress and Female Plumbing

WOMEN with men, women without men, women married, women unmarried, women with women, women alone, women in communes. Sex equals stress. Bad sex equals a lot of stress. Maybe we can use Selye's analysis for sexual tension. Good sex relieves tension. Bad sex aggravates it. Stress and sexuality is a topic of great concern to marriage counselors. They agree that at least 50 per cent of the marriages in the United States suffer from some kind of sexual dysfunction. If you add into that the couples who are living together and those engaged in more casual relationships, you have a very large percentage engaged in an activity that brings them nothing but worry and frustration.

From my days as a marriage therapist, I know that the problems vary: Too much sex, too little sex, too kinky, not kinky enough. All the problems depend on the bag and baggage of norms and values that we bring to a sexual relationship. But not just the kinds of attitudes that we garnered from our mothers and fathers but those attitudes that have been passed down from generation to generation. And as we shall see, the values that have been ripped asunder by mass media in the past fifteen or so years.

A Short History of Sex Therapy

Let us first look at how we are socialized into our sexual attitudes. As products of a puritanical Christian background, we have to look at our historical roots. The early Christian Church reacted against the Jewish and pagan attitudes toward sex. Jews, Greeks, and Romans regarded sex as a healthy indoor activity. Even today, Orthodox Jews believe that religious holidays should be celebrated with sexual intercourse. Since the early Christians were concerned with the imminent second coming of Christ, celibacy was the preferred state. And if you couldn't be celibate, the next best thing was to marry. Remember that Saint Paul said, "It is better to marry than to burn." What Saint Paul meant was that if you couldn't control your own sexual desires, then at least they should be fulfilled within the bonds of marriage. Even though the knights, ladies, and troubadours of the Middle Ages were a bawdy lot, celibacy was still regarded as a preferred and godly state.

In reaction to the licentious Renaissance and the numbers of Princes of the Church who installed their "nephews" in important positions, Luther tacked up his ninety-five theses on the door of Wittenburg Cathedral. The Protestant Church was a reaction against Renaissance hanky-panky. Similarly, the Puritan Church, in England, was a reaction against late-Renaissance hanky-panky. With the accession of Charles II to the English throne and a return to looser morality, the English Puritans sought refuge in the New World. Puritans believed in living a circumspect life, which also meant denial of the flesh and fighting against sexual desires.

Most of us in the United States fall heir to the English Puritan tradition and the later Victorian era. Victoria and her influence among English-speaking countries meant once again a reaction against loose morals and sexual whims and fancies. Today we are well aware that the Victorian era had two sides to it. While sexuality was supposedly repressed and people were taught that babies were born in the cabbage patch, child prostitution, brothels, and sado-masochism also flourished. However, the watchword for the Victorian era was repression.

Repressed nineteenth-century Viennese society was the intellectual breeding ground for Freud. His analysis of childhood sexuality and his emphasis on how sexuality controls human behavior were nothing short of scandalous. Freud's interest in unnatural repression of natural sexual desires seems commonplace enough today but led to his ostracism by the learned doctors of Vienna. Even though many of Freud's analyses of sexuality grate on feminist ears today and in many cases are patently wrong, we cannot deny his contribution to the scientific study of sexuality.

While Freud is undoubtedly wrong in proclaiming that anatomy is destiny and that women are biologically ordained to fulfill themselves in passive roles and in particular in the maternal role, he did rip aside centuries of taboos surrounding sexuality. However, there is an amazing gap between Freud's intellectual analyses and any real laboratory studies on human sexuality. That is what Kinsey found in the mid 1950s, when he began to examine human sexual behavior. Kinsey found that we knew more about animal breeding and the sex life of bees than we did about human sexual behavior. Kinsey, too, suffered the insults and jeers of the public at large and his own academic peers. But Kinsey showed us that there was a wide gap between what people said and thought about sex and what people actually did.

While Kinsey's work still continues at the Kinsey Institute, at Indiana University, it remained for Masters and Johnson to make dramatic breakthroughs in the 1960s in their laboratory research at Washington University, in St. Louis. Today, Masters and Johnson continue their studies in the face of hostility and criticism. The attitude of the late-twentieth century toward sex therapy and research is probably comparable to that of the late-sixteenth century toward the study of physics and chemistry. Those of us brought up to be embarrassed about sex are hard-pressed to look at sex research or sex therapy in an objective and clinical manner.

Therefore we shouldn't be surprised to find that most medical doctors are completely unprepared to deal with the subject of human sexuality. Appendix operations, yes; frigidity, no. The American Medical Association itself was appalled at the results of a survey they sent to medical schools in the early 1960s. The results of that survey showed that of all students on university campuses, medical students had the least knowledge of human sexuality. Medical students were aware of the physiological differences between men and women but were themselves ignorant about the complex interrelationships between men and women and the sexual act itself. Accordingly, most medical schools revised their curricula and spent a portion of lecture time explaining sexual dysfunction and how to deal with patients' sexual difficulties. I was a part-time lecturer in these sessions and am still amazed that young men and women could still giggle over the thought of sexual intercourse.

Many feminists, particularly Barbara Seaman, have written books about male medicine and the difficulties that doctors have in treating women patients. A doctor is usually male and as such has a male viewpoint. This means that he can easily fit a woman patient with a diaphragm or give a woman a prescription for birth-control pills. However, most male doctors have problems dealing with a woman whose dislike of sex is so intense that she vomits at the very thought of intercourse. It may be too much to expect all doctors to be qualified therapists, but we know that most people seek counsel from their physician. Physicians are therapists. Most of them don't do very well.

It's too simple to blame medical failure in the area of sex therapy on the fact that most doctors are men. Some doctors are paternalistic and authoritarian, but not all are.

Probably the male doctor and the female patient are still wrapped up in their puritanical taboos and are simply unable to extricate themselves. Maybe courses on human sexuality in the U.S. medical schools will help future generations of doctors and their patients. But even with increased knowledge and lessened repression, we are still in the Dark Ages. All of us suffer from long-standing taboos. Especially the taboos surrounding menstruation.

Sexuality and Menstruation

For several years, sex researchers and counselors have explored the idea that menarche (the first menstrual period) may forever tinge a woman's attitudes toward sex and her own sexuality. Tribal societies have differing reactions to menarche, just as people of various social classes, ethnic backgrounds, and even regions in the United States do. Mothers around the world instill their sexual attitudes in their daughters at this period. The first menstrual period may be viewed as a crisis or be greeted as a joyous occasion. A mother who reacts with alarm, fear, mistrust, tears, or anger at her daughter's menstrual period will easily convey these attitudes to the young girl. But a matter-of-fact, somewhat clinical attitude combined with pleasure over the daughter's reaching puberty will convey to the young girl the same clinical, matter-of-fact way of dealing with her menstrual period every month.

Let us look at two extreme cases: One mother tells her daughter with tears in her eyes that now she is going to have the "curse." This mother tells the daughter to expect cramping, bloating, at least one or two days in bed, and a life up to age forty-five of monthly misery. Not too surprisingly, the young girl will indeed suffer pain, bloating, and one or two days in bed.

Another mother, when told by her daughter that menstruation has begun, will react without any surprise. Undoubtedly, before this has begun, the mother has engaged in a very long discussion with her daughter as to the virtues of tampons versus sanitary pads. The same mother probably also has bored her daughter with intimate discussions on the physiological aspects of menstruation and pregnancy. The mother does not expect the daughter to have any adverse reactions toward menstruation. The mother will admit that menstruation can be somewhat messy and an annoyance but nothing more than that. As a result, the daughter grows up into a woman who swims, skis, goes to class, teaches school, and rarely takes to her bed during the menstrual period.

I used the foregoing explanation to my women students when I taught courses in human sexuality. I tried to show the women students that cramps and monthly stress could be alleviated by accepting menstruation as a normal—albeit somewhat bothersome—physiological function. Time after time, my female students would come to me after class a month or two after this particular discussion and tell me how they had psyched themselves out of menstrual distress. Usually these girls would recount that they would go back in time to when they were twelve or thirteen or fourteen and had their first period. Then they would analyze their mother's reaction and see whether or not the mother's attitude toward menstruation, sexuality, and body consciousness related to menstrual pain. Sometimes, these women could relate the mother's neutral or pleased attitude to their own pain-free menstrual periods. More often, the women could relate the mother's acute distress to their own menstrual periods, characterized by cramping pain. My success lay in the fact that once these women were able to analyze their own physical distress in relation to their mothers' attitudes, their menstrual pain lessened.

Sometimes I got caught by my own rhetoric. One of my best students came to me one time and confessed that she was unable to take an examination because she had "cramps." I gave her my standard mind-over-matter-mother's-attitudes-sexual behavior-menstrual-cramps lecturette. I warmed to the subject and proceeded to tell her that if she spent two days a month in bed, she would eventually spend a total of three or four years in her whole lifetime in bed nursing her cramps. I waxed even more enthusiastic and told her that I went through graduate school, taught university classes, did consulting work, and wrote books even though I had to withstand some minor menstrual distress. My pomposity was richly rewarded by her amazed comment. Her face lit up and she exclaimed, "YOU! Still! At your age!" So much for role models.

Menstrual Stress and Distress

Talking oneself out of menstrual pain is a lot easier than it sounds. The most common menstrual complaint is dysmenorrhea. Spasmodic dysmenorrhea is also known in the vernacular as "cramping," while congestive dysmenorrhea usually refers to premenstrual tension. Premenstrual distress involves bloating, tension, crying, depression. Study after study has tried to relate menstrual periods to female suicide statistics or to crime rates or to time when women enter psychiatric hospitals and to everything under the sun, including child abuse. The jury is still out. These studies are so badly done and so methodologically impure that no adequate correlation can be made. One thing we do know is that there is a radical drop in estrogen and progesterone levels in the blood immediately before the onset of menstruation.

What we don't know is the effect of these estrogen levels. "Scientific" research shows conclusively that: women are more aggressive before the onset of menses or are more depressed and listless; women have more erotic dreams before the onset of menses or no erotic dreams. We used to be told that women who did not accept the female role were those prone to premenstrual tension, while current research responding to women's liberation now tells us that the androgynous woman, the working woman, or the non-traditional woman has less menstrual tension. There is no firm link between the complications of the hormonal system and emotional responses. Complicated relationships take place between hypothalamus, pituitary gland, and FSH (Follicle Stimulating Hormone). The triggers may be psychological or hormonal or both. With pun intended, this is fertile ground for sex researchers.

Hot baths, cold showers, aspirin, lying on a bed with a cold cloth on top of one's forehead are all ways and means by which women try to alleviate dysmenorrhea. Sometimes an over-the-counter diuretic is sufficient help. A friend of mine has, however, a unique method of dealing with menstrual distress. Since orgasm relieves pelvic congestion, she simply finds herself someone to have long, involved bouts of sexual intercourse with immediately before the onset of her period. The cramping and the premenstrual tension disappear.

A very common menstrual disorder is no period at all, otherwise known as amenorrhea. Young girls away from home for the first time, whether they are at summer camp or the first semester at college, report that they do not have periods. The young women the first year at West Point and in the Air Academy also were amenorrheic. In times of acute and persistent stress a woman's body will react, perhaps in a protective manner. We really don't know. Women during particularly stressful periods become anovulatory. In other words, they do not release, they do not ovulate mid-cycle or release an egg to be fertilized and therefore do not have a period. It's almost as though the body is protecting the woman from having any possibility of conception to avoid either a deformed fetus or even a miscarriage. It's a unique manner of measuring stress among young women.

While there are standard stress measurements for both men and women, such as diarrhea, dry mouth, stomach heaves, clammy hands, headaches, and migraines, some are unique to each sex. Men under acute periods of stress report that they don't have wet dreams, or have difficulty attaining and maintaining erections, and rarely, if ever, wake up in the morning with a full erection. However, with males these are still secondary stress symptoms. How many men are going to admit to problems achieving erection? Women either *do* or *don't* have periods.

Another stress symptom unique to women occurs after

an anovulatory period of several months. Among twenty, thirty, or fifty women, menstrual periods will begin at the same time. This phenomenon is called entraining. Many women recall days at summer camp, weekends living with house maids, or semesters with girls on the same dormitory floor when there was a remarkable coincidence of menstrual periods. Yet, the questions of menstruation, frigidity, blood, body awareness, sexuality, intercourse, conception, pregnancy, and a sense of one's sexual self are all so intricately interwoven that it is hard to separate sexual fantasy from puritanical taboo.

Body Awareness and Nudity

Perhaps because of monthly menstrual periods, women are much more aware of their bodies than men. Of course, girls are socialized to brush their hair one hundred strokes, watch calories, worry about how they look in bathing suits, paint their faces, and above all, use their bodies for the specific purpose of attracting, seducing, and keeping a male meal ticket. Even with our emphasis upon body size and body type, we also are given an unreal physical type for all of us to emulate. Most of us can adjust somehow to the fact that we are not long-legged Scandinavians, with long hair tumbling down our very curvaceous backs. But who doesn't thumb through magazines every spring and wish that her hips were just a little bit smaller?

Some people, however, cannot adjust either to their body weight, body size, or their own nudity. The woman who undresses in a closet is unusual in our society. Yet many men and women have intercourse without the lights on, which is perfectly acceptable. Kinsey connected this custom with social class. In the 1950s, the middle and upper classes made love with the light on and in the nude, while it was entirely lights off and covered for working-class people. Over the past twenty or so years, those statistics have changed but not the general social-class difference between body type, body size, and nudity. In fact it is quite interesting to notice the difference in ideal body types ranging from the Rubensian bodies in *True Detective* to the ghosts of *Vogue.* Given our overemphasis on breasts, narrow hips, long legs, hairless and odorless skin, no wonder every wrinkle is a threat and cellulite a never-ending battle. Madison Avenue constantly bombards every North American woman with the fear that she may be anything from ten to several pounds overweight. Overweight is equated with ugliness and, ultimately, loneliness. A fat woman is not a desirable woman. An undesirable woman would not get a man. At least that's what Madison Avenue tells you.

Rita and the Unending Diet

Rita is a case in point. Rita was a successful real estate saleswoman hamstrung and worried to a frazzle over her body size. Periodically Rita would break out in hives, worrying over whether or not she was too fat. Like most people, she didn't have to worry about being too thin. From the time that she was in high school, Rita was a constant dieter. She knew every diet from the banana-and-skim-milk diet through choking down vegetable oil and some weird kind of protein powder. But Rita worried herself to a tizzy over the question of her physical shape. Until Rita came to her senses, she was obsessed by looking like the models in *Harper's Bazaar* and *Vogue*. And she paid for her psychological obsession with menstrual disorders and sexual difficulties. Rita was one of the exceptions to Kinsey's middle-class rules, because she always insisted on making love with the lights off. The reason was that Rita was ashamed of her small breasts and her somewhat wide hips.

Luckily for her, after a series of live-in and live-out lovers, Rita's (present) husband persuaded her that she was a thing of beauty and would always be a joy to him. A shrewd observer of the social scene, Rita's husband soon discovered her very secret fears. He was the one who convinced Rita that her incessant dieting was unnecessary. The two of them would go through life together; her chest might not get any bigger; her hips might even spread; and Ben—frankly, he didn't give a damn. The moral of this story is not that Rita adjusted to her body size but, through the eyes of a comforting, gentle man she was able to see how she was enslaved by a false concept of beauty.

Prisoners of Our Psyches

Worries that torture us at three o'clock in the morning can twist and distort our lives in such a manner that sexuality is destroyed and personal peace completely undermined. In spite of years of sex psychotherapy and mountains of words written on the subject of frigidity, even in today's sexually aware and supposedly liberated age, frigidity is more than a sometime thing. Frigidity ranges from a woman who dislikes and avoids sex to the very extreme of vaginismus. Vaginismus occurs when a woman is so frightened of sex that her vagina tightens too strongly for intercourse to take place. Perhaps the time and place of the first sexual experience forms an indelible impression on a woman and forever marks her sexual behavior. If you lost your virginity in a quick tussel in the back seat of a Chevrolet at the local drive-in movie, you probably have a rather cavalier, even quite bored attitude toward sex. Rape or incest result in disgust and repugnance. Sexual attitudes and sexual behaviors also stem from parents and church, and most importantly the maternal role model. A new twist in the male-female frigidity battle is taking place. Women are becoming more and more sexually aware in their search for a fulfilling sex life. Beginning, of course, with Freud, continuing through Masters and Johnson, with advice to the lovelorn in newspapers and women's magazines, women are not only becoming aware of but demanding orgasm.

The virtues of vaginal orgasm versus clitoral orgasm have become matters for political debate. For a number of years, sex therapists have been arguing about how many orgasms constitute a multiple orgasm. This increased emphasis on sexuality and sexual liberation is taking its toll—on men as well as women. Men now also have to fulfill multiple roles, both of breadwinner and lover. Not only occasional lover but expert, multiorgasm-producing lover. Women have standards against which they measure their husband's performance. And as we become more liberated, with premarital and extramarital sexual experiences, husbands are measured not only against scales in textbooks but real human beings. Male sexual activity is usually related to economic situation and professional worth. Now that he cannot perform adequately in bed, a husband-lover is more likely to be treated with scorn than with tender, loving sympathy. Some sex researchers, who just happen to be male sex researchers, report that women's sexual demands are probably contributing to male impotency. Women demand fulfillment, orgasms, and most of all multiorgasms. Men must now live up to an impossible standard, whereas prior to today, women had to fulfill a multitude of impossible roles.

Stress and Pregnancy

Women have enough trouble with their own hormonal systems, without having to worry about male impotence as well. While we know that the female body is built specifically for the stress of pregnancy, women's physiology determines the success or failure of conception, pregnancy, and birth. Old wives' tales, studies, fairly detailed observations in lying-in hospitals, and self-reports indicate that highly anxious women have problems conceiving, have high rates of miscarriage, have high incidence of deformed or dead babies, and report difficult labor.

As fear and anxiety increase, so also does difficult labor. Stress, depression, anxiety, and fear are interwoven with the problems of toxemia, pre-eclampsia, excessive weight, and nausea during pregnancy. Psychiatrists used to try to find a relationship between excessive vomiting during the early stages of pregnancy and the mother's desire to rid herself of the baby. Nowadays most psychotherapists view vomiting as a stress *symptom* and not a cause. The maternal role figure may be important in determining a woman's attitude toward her own pregnancy. A pregnant woman's

attitude—acceptance or rejection of the pregnancy and impending birth—directly relates to her own mother's oral
history of pregnancy and birth. The more horrific the tale
the more anxiety is produced. Why not? Ghost stories always entertain children anyway. Since I come from a family in which no woman had less than a twenty-four-hour
labor, no doctor ever saw "such a case in his life," and all
the tales of birth and suffering were embroidered, I find it
hard to envision anything other than impending doom associated with pregnancy and birth. But the matter-of-fact
mother, who matter-of-factly accepts her daughter's first
menstrual period, probably matter-of-factly accepted her
own pregnancy and the birth of a daughter. Interestingly,
women who did not expect pain and suffering at birth are
particularly incensed when they find that these two items
are attendant upon the birth of the baby. We are all aware
of the relationship between nursing mothers and stress and
colicky babies. A mother who is imbued with the La Leche
League ideology and a firm convert to the idea of breast-
feeding a baby may very well be a poor candidate to nurse
her baby. Anxiety produces anxiety. The desire to do right.
The desire to be perfect. The desire to be a warm and nurturant mother. Then what happens? The mother doesn't
produce enough milk; she becomes more anxiety prone; the
milk dries up and the mother considers herself a failure.
And the overanxious, nervous, first-time, obsessive-compulsive new mother can end up with a colicky baby that
screams all night long.

There is firm evidence from laboratory studies that when
pregnant rats are subject to extreme stress such as lack of
sleep or food, flashing lights, etc., the offspring are highly

stressed also. There is some very tenuous link between life-stress events and colicky, restless, upset, nervous, perhaps emotionally disturbed or even autistic children. There are some studies that indicate that pregnancy itself—if it is an unwanted or out-of-wedlock pregnancy—may be stressful enough to produce upset and stressed babies.

However, we must view these correlations with skepticism, because no really long-term studies have followed the stressed mothers and unstressed babies. One person's restless baby may only be another person's happy athlete-to-be daughter. Restless babies do not necessarily grow up to be autistic children or juvenile delinquents. Also, we have to beware of the links between stressed mothers and infant or neonatal mortality.

Poor prenatal care, eclampsia and nutrition deficiency, high rates of miscarriage, and neonatal death are all directly related to both race and socioeconomic class. Socioeconomic class and race often go hand in hand. That is, poor black and brown women usually have poor health facilities, nonexistent prenatal health care, and, obviously, high rates of deformed and dead babies. Anxiety and stress are undoubtedly present here and they are based in reality.

Even though childbirth is a time of crisis and a milestone experience for many women, it is becoming a matter of choice. For middle-class women, not only the spacing and number of children but the very act of conception is one of rational intellectual choice. Given modern contraception, the modern reasonably educated female is now choosing to be a mother, rather than accepting somewhat dubiously an egg conceived after three martinis. The Zero Population Growth people and demographers are delighted in the dipping birth curves since the 1960s. However, in the 1970s something is happening that demographers were unable to forecast: an over-thirty new-mother boom.

Women in their early and mid-thirties who have finished their education and whose careers are reasonably established are now becoming pregnant and having babies. Rather than being mothers in their teens and twenties, educated women today are willingly and somewhat anxiously choosing the mother role before it is too late to conceive. It is to be hoped, as the planned-motherhood people have been telling us for years, every child will be a wanted child or at least a planned child. Suddenly, and not in very large numbers, single women are deliberately choosing pregnancy not associated with marriage. For many women, the mother role is more acceptable than the wife role. What the unmarried mother augurs for the next generation is simply beyond our ken at this particular moment. Let us, however, look at two different case histories.

Adopt and Adapt

Nancy is a woman over thirty who made a rational decision to have a child. The only problem was . . . she couldn't conceive. Nancy and her husband went to every fertility and sterility specialist in the Midwest. To no avail. There seemed to be no physiological problem with either Nancy or her husband. Nancy was afraid that perhaps several years on the pill had rendered her sterile. Her husband's sperm count was adequate. Nothing happened.

Finally Nancy and her husband decided to adopt. They were fast reaching an age when adoption would be impossible. Since there are fewer and fewer white babies available for adoption each year, Nancy and her husband knew that adoption would be difficult. They were one of the lucky ones. True to an old wives' tale, as soon as Nancy adopted, she became pregnant. Nancy had the distinction of being the mother of two children born in the same calendar year. She somewhat ruefully jokes that she really always wanted to have twins but not born ten months apart. Nancy's case is not unusual. What may happen with women like Nancy is that they are so anxious to conceive that their stress/hormonal/endocrine system is in turmoil. The same kind of behavior pattern occurs in an overburdened person who never can complete a task. Stress backfires. So Nancy's body reacts to fight her anxiety over getting pregnant, and she doesn't get pregnant. Once a woman has accepted the fact that she is infertile, and decides to adopt, her stress is correspondingly reduced. Anxiety over fulfilling the mother role is relieved by the act of adoption. Once women have adjusted to the fact that they *never* will become pregnant, that worry disappears. The worry disappears, the stress is reduced, and pregnancy has a better chance of occurring. This does not mean that every case of sterility or infertility can be magically changed and reversed by adoption, only that there are enough cases on record to show the relationship between stress and infertility.

Always Pregnant

Anita is Nancy's polar opposite. Anita is always either pregnant or nursing. Since Anita cannot use the Pill, she is a walking example of continual contraceptive failure. She has a diaphragm baby, a foam baby, a condom baby, and several three-martini babies. Anita truly is superabundantly fertile. She may even be a spontaneous ovulator.

Spontaneous ovulation is an interesting phenomenon and we really don't know if it occurs in women or not. The best-known spontaneous ovulators are female rabbits. While rabbits have a reasonable, well-known, and short ovulatory cycle, they may be spontaneous ovulators. That is, whenever a male rabbit comes in contact with a non-pregnant female rabbit, the female rabbit spontaneously ovulates. And then we all know what happens. At least with rabbits. Anita is not a rabbit, but she may be one of the rare spontaneous ovulators.

Some women do indeed always seem to be fertile and correspondingly always pregnant. Anita is telling the truth when she exclaims, "Whenever he gets near me, I get pregnant!" Anita is always fertile. Or at least she is fertile for a large proportion of her cycle, or she's pregnant.

Abortion—Good, Bad, or Indifferent

While some women desperately try to become pregnant and others can't seem to stop getting pregnant, others view pregnancy as a disaster. Prior to the 1973 Supreme Court decision legalizing abortion, we had no reliable statistics on abortion. By 1976, however, the statistical profile was much clearer. In 1976, doctors performed 1.2 million abortions—one abortion for every 2.8 live births. Ninety per cent of all abortions are performed in the first trimester, and some population experts consider abortion a form of birth control. Seventy-five per cent of the women are unmarried; 67 per cent are white; 20 per cent have already had a previous abortion; 32 per cent are teen-agers; 33 per cent are twenty to twenty-four years old; and 35 per cent are over twenty-five years of age; while 48 per cent have no children, 16 per cent have three or more children.

Abortion foes and abortion supporters hurl invective at each other in the press and on television talk shows; priests and ministers thunder from pulpits, and angry feminists march on Capitol Hill. Organized groups have ensured that massive curtailment of abortion take place in many states. Opponents of abortion quote statistics concerning the emotional strain that having an abortion places on the psyche of a young woman. The evidence is contrary to this assertion.

One of the few dispassionate reviews of abortion statistics and abortion studies, a 1975 report by the Institute of Medicine of the National Academy of Sciences concluded that "the feelings of guilt, regret, or loss elicited by a legal abortion in some women are generally temporary and appear to be outweighed by positive life changes and feelings of relief." Also, additional reports indicate that, since legalized abortion, there has been a dramatic decline in infant mortality, deaths, and complications from illegal abortions, numbers of newborns abandoned for adoption, and rates of illegitimate births. Thus abortion is a stress-relieving mechanism for women who wish to avoid an unwanted pregnancy or the financial and emotional drain of a retarded child. While many of my friends who have had abortions tell me that they regret the pregnancy, regret the strain of the abortion, and have some pang over having had an abortion, they still would repeat the abortion under the same circumstances. Selfish? Maybe. Self-centered? Perhaps. Practical? Yes. Of course, anyone who is morally or ethically or religiously or personally opposed to abortion, and anyone who believes that abortion is tantamount to murder will undoubtedly suffer guilt and psychological stress. But that is the very person who probably wouldn't have the abortion anyway. The stormy arguments pro and con over abortion continue. Yet psychological harm does not accrue, and perhaps psychological well-being results.

Hot Flashes

While we run the full gamut from menarche and subsequent menstruation to conception, pregnancy, and abortion, we finally arrive at menopause. It is a singularly interesting feature of male medicine that there is so little research on menstruation and even less on menopause. Some women have hot flashes, some women don't. Some women experience excruciatingly difficult menopausal periods. Other women do not. Of course, a chemical imbalance occurs in the body. Human beings are among the few animals whose females endure menopause.

Menopause can be in the head, just as menstrual disorders originate in the psyche. There does seem to be a Parkinson's law of female illness. Remember, Parkinson's law states, "Work expands in direct proportion to the time required to fulfill it." My variation on Parkinson's law is "Female troubles are in direct proportion to the time a woman has to enjoy them." Thus, working women have fewer menopausal problems than non-working women. Women simply cannot afford to be ill on the job, but the

STRESS AND FEMALE PLUMBING

housewife can indulge herself in the luxury of illness. Working women may have the same symptoms, but they ignore or surmount them. Since the sick role is acceptable for women, what better way to get sympathy from a spouse or children than by being sick? Bosses are usually not as sympathetic as husbands. Deadlines must be met. Time-cards must be punched.

A very interesting sociological study bears out my Parkinson's law of female troubles. Sociologist Pauline Bart has investigated the empty-nest syndrome, depression, and middle-age women. While she did not specifically study the problems of menopause, her links between depression, middle age, ethnic background, and employment of these women are fascinating. Working women had lower rates of depression than non-working women. While all the women in Bart's sample had children and most of the women had children who had left the home during the previous year, Bart found that the empty-nest syndrome was more serious for non-working women. There were variations among ethnic groups. Jewish women had the highest rate of depression, "Anglos" the next, and blacks the lowest rates of depression. Bart explains that the black women were more likely to be employed outside the home and so were less intensely involved in the home. Thus, black women did not feel the loss of the maternal role as intensely as Jewish women, who were predominantly housewives.

Another adjunct to Bart's study was an extensive search through anthropological files to see how women in over thirty different societies reacted to menopause. Pauline Bart calls herself "the Margaret Mead of menopause." Her results were quite startling. Apparently some societies *re-*

versed their attitudes toward women with the onset of menopause. For example, in societies where women were held in low esteem (such as China), at the onset of menopause, the women were revered in the family setting.

We behave in accord with our cultural taboos. For hundreds of years, we have surrounded all aspects of human sexuality with myth and rituals: birth; menstruation; menopause. Women's rites of passage are mysterious. What is not so mysterious is the way in which women relieve their stress by means of drugs and alcohol.

8

Stress, Drugs, Alcohol, and Food

OBVIOUSLY, any organism can stand only so much stress. Then it will attempt to reduce the stress or die. Stress-reducing mechanisms can be flight, massive inputs of adrenalin . . . or any number of coping mechanisms. Women in the United States use alcohol, drugs, and food as their primary means of coping with stress.

Women are aided and abetted by their male doctors. Male doctors treat their female patients in a superior-subordinate manner. They regard women as silly, funny, flighty creatures whose every whim and slightly neurotic flight of fancy can be masked by a psychotropic prescription. And they may tolerate a female alcoholic because she does most of her drinking at home. Thus male doctors foster female dependency by aiding and abetting the not-so-secret drinker or fostering women's drug addiction. Even the fat woman is another victim. Doctors often prod obese women into more obesity by their constant nagging.

The most important question is why these women choose alcohol, food, sedatives, hypnotic drugs, or sleeping pills in order to see their way through the day. Women patients are easy victims. "That's not me," says the lady doctor, lawyer, teacher, or corporate executive. Only bored, frantic housewives chasing active three-year-olds fall into these traps—not smart young college women on the rise. The statistics show otherwise. Alcoholism, overweight, and drug abuse vary by age, race, and sex, but all socioeconomic groups are affected. There are more male alcoholics than female alcoholics. More women are overweight than are men. More men use and abuse heroin, marijuana, and cocaine than women; but more women use and abuse sedatives, hypnotic drugs, and tranquilizers. Unfortunately, as more women move into the marketplace, more women are inclined to seek unhealthful means to alleviate their stress.

Because of our peculiar socialization, women are unable to adequately give vent to their anger. Men are able to express their anger in a series of violent ways, such as yelling, screaming, banging their fists on tables, or even taking a punch at someone. Women are not allowed this same kind of luxury. As a result, the women tend to push their anger inside and not know how to deal with it. The coping mechanisms that are then most appropriate for the semihysterical woman, the depressed woman, the one who is crying all day long, or the one who is extremely angry at her family is simply to deaden those sensations. Doctors will help by writing a whole series of prescriptions for Equanil and Valium so the housewife can go off in the wild blue yonder. The female alcoholic deadens her anger by getting soused. A woman who blows herself up to a size 24½ calms herself every moment of the day with chocolate fudge and gourmet cheese. Unfortunately, these methods of coping with anger and stress work. They work very nicely. They of course may be counterproductive, because at times they may kill.

Information on women alcoholics and drug addicts is scarce. Few researchers are interested in the poor fat lady. However, recently officials of the FDA became alarmed over the extent of drug addiction among housewives. Thus stricter controls have been instituted regarding uppers and downers given out wholesale by physicians. Women alcoholics are only lately "coming out of the closet."

Women and Alcoholism

Statistics on alcoholism are fuzzy. The National Institutes of Health, the National Institute on Alcoholism, and other organizations quote figures to show that one out of every twelve persons in the United States is an alcoholic. While in years past male alcoholics outnumbered women seven to three, now the figures are closer together. Apparently female alcoholism is on the increase. There are perhaps six male alcoholics to every four women alcoholics. Yet *all* figures on alcoholism are probably *under*-estimates of the real problem. And women alcoholics in particular are more likely to be "hidden" than male alcoholics.

That means that the housewife alcoholic is bound to go undetected, whereas a working man who drinks to excess is seen as a management/supervisory problem. Only a housewife's children and husband know how much she drinks at home. But a worker's foreman and the foreman's supervisor are concerned about his job performance, his absenteeism, and the probability that he will have a serious industrial accident.

Many people who are addicted—to food, alcohol, or pills —simply fit into a disturbed family pattern. One member of the partnership is identified as having a problem, hauled off to jail, dumped in the drunk tank, or put into a sanitarium. Then the whole world knows who the crazy is. But time and time again I have read nurses' notes on patients' charts to the effect that "The husband and not the wife ought to be the patient." Let's look at the case of Alice.

Alice and Alcoholics Anonymous

Alice was a bright, cheery, very intelligent woman. She worked for a large think-tank. She was also an unrepentant and constant drinker. Her job took long hours and she had an exacting boss. Alice learned that a drink with the guys after work helped relieve the tension of the day. A drink while she was preparing for dinner made her often-lonely and lonesome nights more bearable. Alice would often go on dry spells; she wouldn't drink anything stronger than ginger ale.

With her brains and training she was able to hide her alcoholism from everyone at work and in her social life. When things got too bad, she took sick leave. She had bottles stashed all over her apartment. Yet she never went to work drunk, and often without a hangover. She was one of those alcoholics who can literally drink themselves sober. She hid her drinking from everyone around her, including her fiancé, later her husband. She kept her job and drank only at night. Her drinking was never too serious to worry about it. The amount of liquor she consumed was nearly legend in their circles, but she still functioned. At least, she functioned until the baby came. In the midst of a postpartum depression, Alice gave up her job. She seemed to give up everything else as well.

The house was a mess and so was Alice. The baby stank in his dirty diapers. Alice padded around the house in a dirty nightgown no matter what time of day. As the baby grew older, his feeding problems increased. Alice's mother-in-law took the baby every day and tried to help him overcome his finicky eating habits. Alice's husband tried desperately to enlist his mother, Alice's mother, the local minister, friends, work acquaintances—anyone to help talk some sense to Alice. Alice didn't want anyone to talk sense to her. So the husband left. Then the court took the baby. Alice's mother left. Alice was alone. Now Alice had no audience. She had no husband to get upset. She had neither mother nor mother-in-law to rail at her about the dirty house and the uncared-for baby. Alice had no support system. She was too smart and actually too proud to go find a bottle gang to drink with. She knew she was in trouble and she went to Alcoholics Anonymous.

It worked. Why and how AA works is a mystery sometimes even to AA members. If you come to AA kicking and screaming and hauled in by court order or a dour-faced wife or husband, it usually won't work. Alice was lucky in her group. Alice lived in San Francisco and her group were upper-upper-middle-class, well-educated, intelligent drunks. Alice recognized that she was a boozer but she didn't associate herself with those winos in the streets.

When I saw Alice in her sunlit apartment decorated with Marimekko banners and flourishing green plants, I couldn't make a connection between Alice the dirty drunk in the nightgown and this new Alice. Alice and I had gone to graduate school and I was one of the friends that the husband had called in to "talk sense to Alice." Obviously to no avail. The new Alice was holding down a decent middle-management job. Her brains and education had stood her in good stead. All the credit belonged to the AA group, rather than Alice. Alice told me that, the first evening at AA, when she saw the group of well-dressed professionals sitting around a table sipping coffee, she was hard put to remember that it was supposed to be a meeting of AA types. She told me, "When I heard all the nonsense they were giving out about a higher being, about being sober one day at a time, about admitting that you were a drunk, and everything else that they parroted . . . well, I nearly got sick." Well, she probably nearly got sick because she was desperately trying to stay on the wagon, courtesy of her doctor and Antabuse.

She stayed. She met some of the people. She exchanged telephone numbers. She had terrible times. She fell off the wagon. She stopped the Antabuse. She went back to the pills. She stopped going to AA. She returned to AA. She made long-distance calls in the night, ranting and wailing to the, by now, ex-husband. But she survived. She is in her forties now and she survives day by day. She is the exceptionally well-groomed lady you see in the San Francisco upper-upper-middle-class-professional AA group. It is her only support system.

Why did she start to drink? Alice thinks it was the pressures of her job combined with the fact that she was not getting rewards or promotions. Even though her job description meant that she was a low-level analyst, she worked on much-higher-level problems. Her boss criticized her work and took credit whenever she did a good job of analysis or report writing. Even though Alice liked her job, its lack of rewards frustrated her every day. As Alice saw men of lesser ability promoted above her, her anger bubbled inside her.

Once married and quickly pregnant, Alice had a ready-made rationale for quitting the job. Yet she was ambivalent about leaving. She wanted to keep on working but didn't have the courage to look for a higher-paying job. She realizes now that she was in so much conflict over whether to be a career woman or a homemaker that she was unable to see that she could have had the best of both worlds. So anger over giving up her job, anger at herself for not getting another and better job, anger at getting pregnant too soon, and her need to be a perfect mother drove her to drink.

Her life was destroyed, but she is resurrected. She paid a price; so did her husband. The baby is now seventeen years old and can't understand why his mother left him. This young man is justifiably resentful of his new stepmother and the two new babies in the house. He, too, may be a candidate for the bottle brigade in years to come.

New Problems for Old Symptoms

Yet his childhood rejection may lead him into drug addiction. Drug addiction among middle-class kids! Impossible! As we know only too tragically, this new social problem is all too possible. And the problem is growing, as the table below shows.

Percentage of Young Adults who Report "Ever Using"

	18–25 years	Over 26
Marihuana or hashish	60.1	15.4
Hallucinogens	19.8	2.6
Cocaine	19.1	2.6
Heroin	3.6	.8
Alcohol	84.2	77.9
Cigarettes	67.6	67.0

Source: Abelson, Herbert; et al. *National Survey on Drug Abuse: 1977. A Nationwide Study—Youth, Young Adults and Older People. Vol. 1. Main Findings.* Washington, D.C.: National Institute on Drug Abuse, U.S. Department of Health, Education, and Welfare, 1977.

Probably few readers know a junkie. Junkies live on skid row and shoot up with dirty needles. Junkies live in tenements and hide out in alleys. Really? But what if you learned that your next-door neighbor was a junkie, hooked on pills handed out by her physician? More middle-class high school (and over) -educated *females* are junkies than you would realize. Doctors in the United States write more prescriptions for tranquilizers and barbiturates than for ordinary generic prescription drugs. And the majority of these prescriptions are written for *women*.

Remember that we are talking about male doctors with female patients. The sick role is O.K. for women. More women seek medical help than do men. Women actively search out pills—patent or prescription—that offer a magic surcease to real, imagined, neurotic, psychotic, psychosomatic, or hypochondriacal pain. Male doctors often oblige their patients with uppers, downers, or both. Drugged middle-class women have a long history in America. Before the turn of the century, before the passage of the Pure Food and Drug Act, countless numbers of women were using "nerve medicine." Patent elixirs contained high amounts of alcohol or opium. Aunt Tillie lying in a darkened room with a cloth on her head or Grandma nervously opening her bottle of nerve medicine were hidden addicts.

Today, housewives can't buy opium and morphine or cocaine over the counter, so they have to go to their own family physician in order to get drugs. Sadly, many women who cluck over teen-age drug addiction, worry over the powerful effects of LSD, tut-tut over the evils of marijuana, and become spastic over mentioning the evils of cocaine, are themselves addicted. Their addiction is Valium, Dalmane, Equanil, or Miltown, all perfectly acceptable in Scarsdale and Grosse Pointe. Actually, Equanil and Valium are perfectly acceptable anywhere in middle America. "The doctor gave me something for my nerves" is repeated on the farm, in the suburbs, and in the big-city high-rise. The "something for your nerves" may end up killing you, or it can ruin your life psychologically. Addiction is not a pleasant thought. Yet it can happen easily, as Betty Ann found out.

Betty Ann and Darvon

Betty Ann saw the ravages of pill-popping every day on duty at a private mental hospital. She knew what could happen to people who innocently got hooked on prescription drugs. She knew that of all professional groups in the United States, doctors and nurses are most prone to drug abuse and drug addiction. The explanation is quite obvious: these are people who have access to drugs. But that really is too facile an explanation, because dentists, veterinarians, pharmacists, and various researchers have access to drugs as well. However, hospital life, emergency-room drama, postoperative shock, and all the soap-opera elements of a large hospital are more traumatic for physicians and nurses when compared to dentists and veterinarians. Doctors and nurses are addicts much more often than their counterparts in other professions that deal in drugs.

Even though Betty Ann knew all these statistics and had attended the drug-prevention seminars in the hospital, she thought she would never get hooked. Just like the cigarette smoker who reads the label on the cigarette package about cigarette smoking and cancer, Betty Ann was convinced that she was immune to any drug problem. A widow with two active, busy preteen-agers, Betty Ann somehow made it through long days and even longer, lonelier nights. When her husband died, Betty Ann returned to work to keep the house and make sure that the children stayed in their own, familiar neighborhood. Betty Ann took the graveyard shift—eleven at night to seven in the morning—because she could run her house around those hours. She could be home for breakfast and see the children off to school. Do a few household chores and get some sleep and be at the house when the children returned from school. The problem was that she didn't get enough sleep.

Betty Ann worried about money, about being too harsh, too lenient, about leaving the children alone in the house at night, about the house burning down, and about a whole series of things that left her tossing and turning. Trying to sleep in the daytime wasn't easy. The light kept filtering in through the cracks in the windows and she kept worrying and worrying. So Betty Ann didn't sleep.

Although Betty Ann's eleven-to-seven shift was relatively easy, she still reeled from being so tired. She sometimes tried to catch a little nap while sitting at her desk, but that never worked out. She was afraid of getting caught and being fired on the spot. A couple of times, the nurse's aides covered the desk while she went off to the ladies' room and tried to get an hour's sleep. Nothing worked. She didn't sleep during the day, she couldn't cat-nap at work. Betty Ann was bone-tired all the time.

One night, she was chatting with one of the doctors who had come on to check one of his patients. Dr. Van Dorn worked phenomenally long hours too. Surgery at seven and ward rounds up to eleven o'clock at night. Van Dorn listened patiently to Betty Ann's complaints and then he suggested a shot of Darvon to help her relax. He told Betty Ann that Darvon was the only thing that kept him going and enabled him to get through his twenty-hour days. Betty Ann agreed. She should have known better. She knew that doctors and nurses were prime subjects for the middle-class-addiction syndrome. She knew that Darvon was the favorite drug for the nurse/doctor junkie. Why did she agree with Van Dorn?

She agreed because she was tired, and desperate. Besides, she was too smart to get hooked, because she knew all the pitfalls. At the same time, she trusted Dr. Van Dorn. He didn't look like a junkie and he used Darvon all the time. So Betty Ann, Dr. Van Dorn, and the needle became linked in an unholy triangle. Before Betty Ann left the hospital, Van Dorn would slip up to her floor and would sign an order for Darvon for one of his patients. Obviously the patient didn't get the shot, but Van Dorn and Betty Ann split the ampule and shot up in the drug room. Nobody knew. Nobody found out. The hospital pharmacist and the narcotics-control people kept tabs on all the drugs and medicines in the hospital. Both sides of the drug sheets balanced out. So many ampules of Darvon distributed to the nursing-ward drug rooms and so many given out to the patients. No discrepancies anywhere to worry anybody.

Betty Ann surely wasn't worried. After a while, it really was immaterial if Van Dorn did or did not write orders for Darvon. Betty Ann got sneakier and sneakier at getting her own source. If she was to give a patient a shot, the patient didn't get a full 50 cc's but got, say, 45 cc's. It didn't make *that* much difference to the patients, yet it was super important to Betty Ann! She never went as far as some nurse-addicts and fill syringes with water and palm the ampules of Darvon to get the full amount. Though she probably would have reached those depths.

Betty Ann faced a life of addiction, theft, jail terms, and a disintegrating home life. If she thought she was tired before Darvon, she was worse after starting to take it. She got through the day and the long nights, but she paid a price. Betty Ann thought she was too smart to get hooked, but she was smart enough to realize that she was a Darvon junkie. Her kids floated past her eyes; the housework did not get done; the patients' complaints floated around in the air, and even Betty Ann floated around. Finally, Betty Ann decided that she had to stop this nonsense and get some help. She sought out one of the hospital staff psychiatrists and confessed all. Luckily, he did not report her to the administration.

Dr. Anderson told Betty Ann that her problems were indeed overpowering but that she had to see her way out. The house was too big for a single woman to maintain on a reduced salary; the children were far too young to leave alone every night—in case of fire, theft, or whatever; Betty Ann's physical makeup probably would never adjust to the crazy graveyard shift; and Betty Ann was a junkie. Only Van Dorn and Anderson knew. Betty Ann had covered her tracks well enough and had not become so incapacitated that she had been discovered. Anderson and Betty Ann worked out a plan of action to reconstruct her life. It worked.

First, Betty Ann borrowed enough money to send the kids to an all-summer camp, and courtesy of Blue Cross, Betty Ann went to her own version of summer camp. Rather than flies and mosquitoes of her children's summer camp, Betty Ann's drug rehabilitation program included creatures on the walls that no one but Betty Ann could see. She survived, and she kicked her addiction cold turkey: quick and painful withdrawal. The children came home from summer camp and found a tired, rather gaunt mother who put their house up for sale. The house was sold with a substantial profit. Betty Ann and her children moved into a large, roomy apartment building, and Betty Ann gave up the graveyard shift and began to work (for less money) for a general practitioner. The kids adjusted. Betty Ann went back to school a few nights a week and got her master's degree. She now teaches nursing at a local community college. Her salary has doubled and her worries have been halved. Her stress was relieved and she became a success story of coping. Not, however, before she had hit rock bottom.

Most addict stories are not successes but modern-day Faustian mad descents into hell with no way back. Betty Ann's problems were reality-based. She was a widow without enough money who was trying desperately to maintain a life style that was impossible to continue. Rather than limiting her scope, she pushed herself beyond endurance, until she needed a crutch to help her survive. The crutch became a club. Betty Ann had enough sense, gumption, experience, fear, or blind luck to admit that her addiction was a killer. She not only had the sense to admit her failures but the stamina to withstand the physical torment of a drug withdrawal. Not too many people can do that. Not too many people can revise and revamp their lives in a healthy, constructive manner. Betty Ann did and she was lucky. However, the experience scared Betty Ann nearly out of her wits. There are other forms of addiction that don't scare people but destroy lives equally as well.

Food Addiction

Food also can be an addiction. Weight Watchers and other diet clubs such as Overeaters Anonymous are based on that premise. Some psychoanalytic theorists attribute overeating to a childhood "oral fixation." Freud wrote that people pass through oral, anal, and genital stages. As the result of trauma, some people get stuck in the oral stage. Just like the baby who has to stick his fingers, toes, and Teddy bear into his mouth, so there are lots of people who suck on pencils, bite their nails, stuff their mouth with chocolate cake, or suck on a wine bottle. They are orally fixated. Pleasure comes to the body via the mouth. Sucking on your Teddy bear's ear is fun and rewarding at three years old, so stuffing your face in midnight raids on the refrigerator is psychologically rewarding at thirty-three years old. Drugs and booze have a shabby, tawdry, skid-row, hippie, communie aura about them. Chocolate cake is quite innocuous. But chocolate cake and pasta can kill physically and maim psychologically just as terribly as vodka or heroin. Overweight is a serious health problem for women in the United States.

If we could solve the problems of the food junkies, we'd all be millionaires like Jean Nidetch, of *Weight Watchers* fame. Nidetch and *Overeaters Anonymous* adopted the credo and manner of Alcoholics Anonymous meetings. Every member is an addict. Every member is entitled to backslide and return again to the fold. Every member will live only one day at a time and fight her food addiction one day at a time. No magic panaceas, no pills, no super protein powders, no nothing. Sheer will power peels the pounds off and keeps them off. That is, if you want to get them off. The tragedy of most food addiction (like alcoholism and drug addiction) is that the victim enjoys her victimization. At least Marilyn did.

Marilyn and Her Fat Cells

Marilyn is a classic case of an overweight woman who uses her overweight as a means of punishing herself, protecting herself, and punishing all the members of her close family circle, and uses her food addiction for coping and control. A slim young bride with a patrician face, Marilyn became, within two years of her wedding day, a sullen, two-hundred-pound lump of jiggling fat. What happened to the radiant bride? Marilyn explained her problem away by a long treatise on fat cells and how her whole endocrine imbalance had been thrown out of kilter by her pregnancy. Maybe the fat-cell story was true, but there seemed to be no medical basis for Marilyn's overweight. However, the pregnancy and Marilyn's subsequent obesity were indeed yoked together.

Even though Marilyn was not a virgin when she and Edward got married, she had had very limited sexual experience. Her experiences with intercourse involved a lot of fumbling around in the back seat of cars, quick penetration, and then nothing. Marilyn was not orgasmic. She really didn't enjoy sex at all. She let Edward take her to motels for some sweaty jumping up and down on creaky beds, because she was pretty well convinced that if she didn't let Edward have sex, he wouldn't marry her. Edward thought Marilyn was as good a sex partner as he had had in a long time. Plus she was neat, clean, obviously well educated and would make a good wife. They would get married.

Edward didn't take the time to find out whether Marilyn enjoyed sex or not or if she had reached orgasm. His sex life was good. He had sex with Marilyn every night from the first night of the honeymoon. Marilyn used a diaphragm, but one night she either forgot it or didn't put it in properly and she got pregnant. The baby was born exactly nine and a half months after Marilyn and Edward walked down the aisle. Marilyn was furious when she found out that she was pregnant. She knew that she didn't want to have a baby and become a mother before she and Edward really knew each other. For Marilyn, sex was a nasty business which led to a distended, bloated belly and morning sickness. That's what sex was all about. Grudgingly, Marilyn accepted her pregnancy and began to eat for two.

Actually, Marilyn began to eat for three or four people. The obstetrician warned her about putting on too much weight, but Marilyn kept on eating. She ate and ate and ate with the maniacal fury of a caterpillar munching through a bower of petunias. She grew bigger and fatter, day by day. Her ankles got bigger and her face grew rounder. She told Edward that they shouldn't have sex because of the baby, and because she felt lousy anyway and wouldn't enjoy it. On the rare occasions when Edward made a feeble attempt, the sex was awful. So he stopped making any attempts. He worried about the baby and was looking forward to its arrival.

After the baby was born, Edward thought, he would get back to the honeymoon once-a-night routine with his chic little sexy wife. She was no longer chic, hardly sexy, and had turned into a mountain of woman. Marilyn made no attempt to go on a diet or engage in an exercise program. She threw herself into her mother role with a vengeance. Even though she secretly resented the baby for the life-style and physical changes that she had wrought, Marilyn decided her little girl would be the cleanest, brightest little baby in the whole block, or maybe the whole country.

Marilyn cleaned, shined, scrubbed, sewed, embroidered, and knitted for her charming little baby. The baby's room was like a replica of a nursery-rhyme illustration of the princess' baby's room. Drooped and draped gossamer curtains surrounded the bassinet. The room abounded with dozens of little dolls and stuffed toys. The mother was the only disparate note. Marilyn dressed in garish colors, although all of her dresses faintly resembled her maternity dresses. Muumuus and caftans scarcely hid the hulking figure below the flowing fabrics.

Although Marilyn was no longer pretty, no one could accuse her of being a bad mother. She was more of a mother than a wife, although her baked goods and gourmet meals for Edward were becoming something of a legend in the neighborhood. Edward got the message very quickly. He got rebuffed when he made his attempts at sex. Marilyn used the classic "I'm too tired" routine. Headaches, back-aches—anything was a reasonable excuse for Marilyn to avoid sex. But Edward hated the thought of having sex with a lumpy whale. He redirected his sex drive. He occasionally patronized a bordello, and masturbated a lot. After a while, though, Edward discovered that there were many young girls in his office who liked sex for its own sake and were not amiss to taking him to their apartments for sex on the noon hour. It was a long-standing joke about Edward and his "nooners."

Marilyn didn't think it was so funny when one of her very best friends told her about Edward's extracurricular activities. She faced him down with her suppositions and accusations and he crumbled. Quite obviously, neither Edward nor Marilyn wanted a divorce. Each one had adjusted to symbiotic misery. Marilyn had deliberately made herself ugly to avoid Edward's sexual advances. Edward felt guilty about making Marilyn too pregnant too soon. He also felt guilty about hating Marilyn's ugly body. Then the guilt was increased a thousandfold when Marilyn found out about the girls at the office. Edward became the sinner, Marilyn a saint.

In the arguments that followed, Edward railed at Marilyn about her excessive eating and not caring about her appearance. Whereupon Marilyn made excuses about her fat cells, her endocrine imbalance, the pregnancy, the toll of her twenty-four-hour labor, and the worry about the baby, the house, the mortgage, and so on. Marilyn couldn't help being fat.

Fun and Games

Marilyn *could* help a lot of things, but she and Edward were locked into a dependent relationship that they both enjoyed. Most addicts, whether or not the addiction is food, drugs, or alcohol, have willing partners to support their habits and their personality quirks. The junkie's mother is distraught when the child steals money from her purse to buy drugs. The therapist asks why the mother left the purse in full view with more money in the wallet than the mother usually carries with her. Possibly the mother is unconsciously fostering the child's drug habit so that he will be forever dependent on the good wishes and dole of the strange mother.

Sometimes the spouses cannot stand the attempts of the husband or wife to rehabilitate himself or herself. Bizarre patterns emerge. A wife who successfully loses weight with Weight Watchers is puzzled when her husband begins to bring home cake, pizza, and beer. When a husband stays on the wagon courtesy of Alcoholics Anonymous, he is mystified when his wife begins to drink to excess.

The explanations are painfully obvious to the outside observer. These marriages survive only when one spouse is chained by guilt, dependency, money, hate, or whatever to the other. In these marriages the superiority-inferiority positions may shift and change over time, but one thing is clear: neither the addicted spouse nor the long-suffering-martyr spouse wants to change things. Each person in this neurotic relationship willingly becomes victim or persecutor. And they tolerate extremely high stress levels. One or both of the partners may end up dead with cirrhosis of the liver or a heart attack.

Joan and Diet Pills

Joan is a case of multiple addiction: pills, alcohol, and food were all used to relieve stress. A good cook and an even better eater, Joan was obsessed with food. She bought cookbooks, she haunted gourmet restaurants, she collected recipes in overflowing accordion files, and she was a sure pushover for any kitchen gadget advertised on TV. She was very fat. And she was not very nice.

Her life was circumscribed by her weight. Joan didn't dare take baths, because she was afraid of getting stuck in the tub. She slept downstairs, because she couldn't manage the stairs to the second story. Joan was afraid of taking the subway, as she might get stuck in the turnstile. Museums, art galleries, expositions, or fairs were simply out of the question, because Joan could only shuffle and waddle slowly before finding a bench to sink down on. As she was well aware, children giggled as she waddled past; she was fiercely jealous of every slim person in the world, and her life became more and more unbearable.

She was literally an agoraphobic—a person who is afraid to leave her house. Why should she leave her comfortable house? The husband did the shopping, cleaned the house, did general repairs, and asked only to be left in peace to watch TV and read a little. The daughter did the laundry and tidied up, too. The daughter wanted only to retire at night to her books. Joan had her food and everything was all right. That is, everything was all right as long as Joan determined that it was. Otherwise, Joan would throw tantrums and fits that would terrorize the daughter and the husband. Joan could become violent, punching and pounding her husband and child.

This family pattern continued for years and years. The husband didn't want too much of a life outside of his own office, either. The fact that Joan was a prisoner inside her own body who hid inside her house was fine with him. He had a low sex drive and his television programs were all that mattered. The daughter was different. As she grew older, she realized that the life she thought was normal was actually abnormal. The more she saw of her girlfriends' homes the more she realized that her mother was disturbed. Sadly the daughter realized that her father was different from other people as well.

When the daughter went away to college, she didn't return. She got summer counseling jobs and then a fellowship and then simply never came back. Joan screamed and cried for days. Her servant had disappeared without so much as a thank you. Things were now worse for the husband, because he had additional household chores. Slowly at first, but increasingly, he began to complain to Joan. Then he went away. Joan was now truly frantic. She had to take the bus instead of sitting like a glowering Buddha in the back seat of the family car. She had to lug her tons of groceries home all by herself. She had to go to divorce court and hear the husband and the daughter say terrible things about her.

So she decided that she would show everybody up. She would go on a diet. She went to a famous diet doctor who prescribed rainbow pills and gave her diuretic shots and several magic diets. These worked like the proverbial abracadabra charm. Joan's pounds did go away. So did some of what was left of her sanity. Previously Joan had not been too stable, but with rainbow pills and not sleeping, she became worse. Joan wandered around her empty house night after night trying desperately to get to sleep. She wanted to lose weight, for she was convinced that the husband and the daughter would come back and life would be beautiful. No such luck. One night, she was so frantic for sleep that she poured herself a large glass of bourbon. She never woke up.

Heal Thyself

What do these unhappy case histories tell us? Female alcoholism is on the rise. Psychotropic drugs such as Valium and Equanil are widely used by housewives. Harried male and female executives gulp uppers and downers by the handful. Obesity prevents women from obtaining or keeping good jobs—and can destroy lives as effectively as the bottle of liquor or pills. Stress kills via an intermediary. Stress produces tension. Pills, food, or liquor alleviates the tension. Thus booze, chocolate cake, or Miltown becomes an addiction. The addiction produces physical cravings and reactions. Sometimes death results.

Addiction is an evil stress-alleviating mechanism. Jogging, Transcendental Meditation, gardening, church activities—these are healthful substitutes to ease unbearable tensions. Another, more effective method, is to cut down on some of the tension-producing areas in your life. Your husband is unbearable; divorce him. Your job is boring; find a new one. Be sure to find a method of coping that is healthful and reasonably non-stressful.

When one of my psychotherapist-consultant friends asked me in an open session how I coped with my 712 stress points on the Holmes and Rahe scale, I told him without thinking, "I change my hair color a lot." And that was really not a Freudian *gaffe*. My tension-relieving mechanism is to find a hairdresser and sit under the dryer and hide for an hour or two. I look on hairdressers-beauticians-cosmeticians as therapists. After all, the hair stylist works on the head too, and charges much less. Shopping is another feminine method of tension relief. But there are many others.

Consider the popularity of religious retreats at Catholic monasteries or convents—for non-Catholics as well as Catholics. Zen retreats. Yoga weekends. Quaker meditations. We all have a need for a quiet time to reconsider and re-evaluate. Or, better yet, to sleep late and do nothing. One young couple I know have a nice working arrangement with another couple who are also young parents. Two or three times a year, one couple get the kids, while the other couple check into the local Holiday Inn for breakfasts in bed and afternoon swims in the heated pool. It is a mini-vacation within the family budget and close enough for any emergency. It also works.

But if you have a more serious problem, such as alcoholism or drug addiction, there is a whole network of support and help. Alcoholics Anonymous works. Al-Anon helps the teen-ager and the spouse. Drug rehabilitation programs within industry and attached to community mental health centers have eager and capable staffs. Weight Watchers is a financial success because it is the most spectacular and effective method of losing weight. The remedies are at hand, if you or your spouse or child or employee wants to take advantage of them. But it is hard to rid oneself of one's own favorite neurosis, or crutch. Helplessness and dependency mean that someone is around to take care of helpless little old you. Growing up is a painful experience, whether accomplished at age sixteen or thirty or fifty. Sometimes people need help in achieving maturity. Psychotherapy sometimes helps.

9

Stress and
Mental Illness

UNFORTUNATELY, in the United States women outnumber men as far as mental illness is concerned. Psychiatrists and psychotherapists report their patient census runs four to five women to every male patient. A higher number of women enter state or private psychiatric facilities. There is historical precedent for women exhibiting more stress symptoms than men. Even Freud, at the turn of the century, had a greater proportion of women patients than men. The favorite illness of the Vienna of the 1900s was involutional hysteria. The word hysteria comes from the Greek word *hysterikós*, meaning "of the womb." Linguistically there is some connection between having a

womb and being an excitable, wild, uncontrollable personality. People who have wombs—i.e., women—are thought
to be unstable and inferior. Perhaps, then, women in the
Western world are encouraged to have more mental problems than men.

Mental illness respects neither social class nor race, but
the sex differences are pronounced everywhere. Statistics
from the Army (Walter Reed Hospital) show that enlisted
women have a higher percentage of psychiatric symptoms
than do men. The Naval Research Personnel Center
affirms that navy women are treated much more often for
psychiatric problems than navy men. One very disturbing
statistic also shows that while, of all professions, doctors
commit suicide at the highest rate, women doctors kill
themselves at a rate three times higher than men doctors.
Male therapists and even female therapists agree that
women break down faster and easier than men. Phyllis
Chesler writes that doctors are much more prone to give
women prescriptions for tranquilizers, treat them for hysteria, keep them in long-term therapy, and generally foster
the sick role. However, the sick role may also be seen as
good preventive medicine. Women do seek therapy in a
greater proportion than do men; when men are admitted to
psychiatric hospitals, they have been sicker longer. Most of
our data come from large state psychiatric hospitals and are
suspect. However, these data indicate that men are more
likely to be more seriously disturbed, are hospitalized for
longer periods of time, are released with less frequency, and
are more prone to violence. Men think being sick is a sign
of weakness. Tradition says that women are weak. So, obviously, a woman will not be diminished in her sexual iden-

tity if she admits to a slight neurosis or feelings of deep depression.

Women, then, can give in to their illness or at least try to seek adequate medical-therapeutic relief. As we know, all is not a bed of roses. While the sick role means that women do seek therapy and help, the kind of help they get is usually inadequate. Of course, most mental therapy in this country is inadequate anyway, but that is a personal opinion.

The Therapy Game

The first thing one should remember on entering therapy is that therapy is a gigantic game. In transactional analysis there is a game called Victim-Rescuer-Persecutor. Somebody decides that he wants to be rescued, because he is a victim. He finds himself a rescuer to release him from whatever terrible person is doing the persecuting. The therapist can play both roles and can play any role, as can the client. The therapist, for example, is the rescuer who sometimes takes the persecutor role, pounding on the patient, who usually is the victim. When the patient doesn't behave, then the therapist becomes the victim and the patient the persecutor. In this portion of the game the therapist says, "If you only did what I told you to do you would be a perfect person." Then the patient becomes the persecutor, arguing, "I did what you told me to do and it's very painful."

Most of the time, however, the therapist-client-psychiatrist-patient relationship is that of superordinate versus subordinate. The client takes advice and the therapist gives it.

The therapist is all-knowing, all-wise, and omnipotent. As Phyllis Chesler and others point out, this unfortunately is not always the case. Anne Seiden describes the therapist-client relationship as "one-down." She points out that women are placed in subordinate positions by seeking help and they gratefully remain in a supplicant state throughout therapy. This is a replay of the Victim-Persecutor-Rescuer theme: I give advice. You take advice. You do not take my advice. Therefore, you are a bad person.

I remember the shock effect of Betty Friedan's *The Feminine Mystique* upon college-educated women of the nineteen sixties. This was the group that had swallowed the home-hearth routine and followed the advice of Neo-Freudians that a woman's role was that of cultured, dignified helpmate forming the next generation. However, psychotherapists' offices were filled with these neurotic suburban matrons. Somebody benefited: the banks and the psychotherapists. If Freud was right and biology is destiny, then an unfulfilled woman ought to have another baby, and another, and another.

Then the silent and soon vociferous social movement began. Women slowly began to return to work and school. Tentatively at first, then in waves, women began continuing-education courses and then became full-time students. New demands and new critiques were heard. Women psychotherapists challenged Freud and his followers. Karen Horney's work on the psychology of women and the self-affirmation of woman's identity came back into prominence. Women psychologists and women psychiatrists attacked the principles of psychotherapy. Cries of "personhood" were heard throughout the land. Just as women objected to television programs and children's stories that always portrayed women as dumb, defenseless, passive creatures, so women psychotherapists said that passivity, masochism, dependence, and depression were not attributes peculiar to women.

Blame the Victim

Things may be getting better, but women have a long way to go before they reach intellectual parity with the therapeutic—male—community. While researching this chapter, I came across a 1977 article by a prominent British physician that is so pernicious I could scarcely believe what I was reading. John Pollitt presents a sensible and reasonably thorough overview of male-female sex differences. He correctly assesses the state of the art and concludes that there are few intellectual differences between men and women. However, Pollitt points out that the only real difference between men and women is the fact that women menstruate and men do not. The "crisis" and the physical strain of menstruation account for women's high rate of psychiatric illness and for the fact that more women are diagnosed as depressed than men. Here is a direct quote:

> As depressive illness is so much commoner in women between 15 and 45, menstruation, pregnancy, the puerperium and the menopause may account for their vulnerability.

Pollitt uses badly researched findings to support his contention that *all* female problems result from the menopause. He even shows that menstruation is responsible for the fact that women can't commit suicide with the same efficiency as men:

Perhaps one reason for the female's lack of success [in sui-
cide] is that the majority of attempts are made during the
premenstrual phase or menstruation. Killing oneself is not
easy; success requires careful planning. Women in the premenstrual phase show a marked tendency to be careless,
thoughtless, unpunctual, forgetful or absent-minded (they
are more likely to be involved in motor accidents and de-
tected in crime). This inefficiency at a time when they are
more likely to end their lives may result in their dispropor-
tional failure.

With dispassionate and objective friends of women like
Pollitt, who needs any more enemies? Women menstruate
and therefore they are thoughtless, unpunctual, forgetful,
or absent-minded. Yet Mother Nature protects us. Our
menstrual or premenstrual symptoms make us so careless
and ineffectual that we can't kill ourselves. Remember this
1977 article when you are choosing a psychotherapist, some
of whom may share the same underlying assumptions.

Finding a Psychotherapeutic Fit

Just as very few people can tell the difference between
ophthalmologist and optometrist, most people don't know
the difference between psychiatrist and psychologist. I
would opt for a psychiatrist. A psychiatrist, remember, is a
person who has received a degree of M.D. and then studied
four additional years interning in the field of psychotherapy. Thus, the psychiatrist should be able to find any
neurological, biological, or biochemical imbalance that
may have triggered a psychiatric mental breakdown. On
the other hand, there are good therapists who are psychol-

ogists. Unfortunately, licensing of psychologists can vary from state to state and sometimes even within states. Seeking a psychotherapist is like looking for a good hairdresser. It's an art more than a science. Most states only require that psychologists have a master's degree. I would hold out for at least a Ph.D. and some interning experience. Some jurisdictions allow an unqualified person to hang out a shingle on the front of his house. He may advertise in the yellow pages and collect money from an unsuspecting public—usually a female public. Remember, you should choose your psychotherapist as you do your hairdresser. If you don't get good service, go elsewhere. There is such a thing as psychiatric fit.

The major reason why I recommend psychiatrists over psychologists is their emphasis upon the physical and biochemical. Many psychiatrists focus on the emotions at the expense of the body. Your psychiatrist should first order a top-to-bottom physical examination. He probably won't do this himself but send you to a reasonably good internist. Or you can find a good internist yourself and see if there is anything physically wrong first, before you begin therapy. There are problems such as brain tumors, diabetes, hormonal imbalance, etc., that produce aberrant behavior. While hypoglycemia has become the chic illness of the past few years, there is no reason to doubt the mounting evidence of the link between hypoglycemia and rather strange behavior.

Which now brings up another point. Cocktail-party chit-chat and college sophomores will usually regale you with the phrase "Nobody knows what normal is, anyway." That is absolute nonsense. We do have standards of normal behavior. When someone starts screaming with hate, railing at the world, flailing with fists, and, in general, losing control, we know that is not normal. A woman who shuts herself up in her house for days at a time and loses all sense of proportion—she's not normal either. If your hands shake a great deal and you have the dry heaves, that's not normal. Neither is normality associated with chronic insomnia or agoraphobia (the fear of leaving the house). Once a person ceases to function, then she is no longer normal. Now, some families can tolerate a woman lying on a couch in a darkened room with a cold cloth on her forehead, sniffing smelling salts and having a case of the vapors. That usually belongs to Tennessee Williams plays and not real life. Depending upon your station in life, however, perhaps this behavior can be tolerated. As women enter into the work force, this kind of withdrawing, depressive behavior is unacceptable. More women are single-parent mothers and of necessity are forced to function under conditions of great stress. Even the idea of living life through tranquilizers is no longer acceptable to the working woman/mother.

So women seek surcease.

Beware of the Chemical Gift

As previously discussed, relief via tranquilizers and sleeping pills is dangerous indeed. At the risk of sounding like a homeopathic nut or a Christian Scientist railing against modern inventions, let me repeat, Beware doctors bearing chemical gifts. Just as the TV commercial announces, "It's not nice to fool around with Mother Nature," so also we must remember that once the gods give the gift they exact payment. We have seen, for example, that there are behavioral disruptions directly associated with the birth-control pill. God only knows what the long-term effect of Red Dye Number 2 has been, not only upon our bloodstream but our head. A terribly serious problem for many women is not only addiction to, but psychiatric illness directly attributed to the use of, sleeping pills. We researchers and psychotherapists know one basic fact: dreaming is necessary for mental health. Nightmares, dreams in color, erotic dreams, wet dreams, funny dreams—these are methods for sorting out the past day's problems and the next day's schedule. How many times have you gone to bed very disturbed over a problem, tossed and turned, sworn that you never slept at all, and got up the next morning with the solution for the previous evening's trouble? Probably quite a few times. Sleep researchers know that a person is dreaming by fluttering of the eyelids, also known as REMs (Rapid Eye Movements). When a person takes sleeping pills, he *does not* dream. There are no REMs. Thus there is no sorting out of inner problems and outer difficulties. Nonetheless, dreaming is of prime importance for mental health. No REMs, no dreams, lots of problems. If you don't dream at night, the odds are that you are going to hallucinate during the day. Thus we see that there is a direct link between overuse of sleeping pills and mental illness. Once again, the gods have exacted their price. How strange it is that the human spirit can become discombobulated through overuse of sleeping pills and soar to magnificent heights in time of war.

Survival Is the Game

One of the mysteries of the psychotherapeutic community is how one woman is able to endure long periods of pain or the sheer unspeakable horror that was Dachau, Auschwitz, or Ravensbrück, while another woman, in a North American suburb, breaks down in the face of teenage suburban rebellion. One story that impressed me most belongs to a dear, seventy-year-old, gray-haired, tiny woman from Belgium, Mme. Jaqueline engaged in underground activities in Belgium and Holland during the Second World War. She recounted her activities in a comfortable western Maryland suburban home in front of a fire, while sipping cognac. Slowly and hesitantly, she told how she had been the kingpin of Belgian resistance, and had arranged the escape of downed British and Canadian flyers and transmitted information. After she was betrayed by a collaborator of the Nazis, she was tortured in two Nazi fortresses and then sent to the infamous women's concentration camp of Ravensbrück. Quietly she told of rape, torture, medical experimentation, ashes raining down on the camp, and the smell of burning human flesh. She was one of the lucky ones expatriated by Count Bernadotte of Sweden. The train carrying over four hundred women resistance prisoners from Holland, Belgium, and France slowly wended its way to Sweden. The Nazis methodically bombed the well-marked rescue train. Of some four hundred women who left Ravensbrück, scarcely a hundred and eighty arrived in Sweden, and of those, only a handful survived.

This gallant lady is not bitter; she did survive, as did many thousands like her. She lost her lands and bank account to the rapacious collaborators and Nazis. But her soaring spirit and her inestimable bravery were an inspiration to her daughter, her family, and her nation. How many of us can say the same?

It is so easy to focus on maladjustment and craziness, rather than on adaptation. Perhaps it is this American mania for introspection that leads women down the path of madness. Sinking into insanity is probably very easy. It is chic to have a therapist. It is socially acceptable to pop pills. Sometimes at cocktail parties you feel that if you haven't had a breakdown you really don't count. One friend of mine who was on the Democratic National Committee recounts a story about Senator Eagleton that is quite amusing, although extremely ironic. He tells how many of them knew that Eagleton had had shock treatment and in-depth psychiatric therapy. But as he says, "We were all New York Jews and we had all been in therapy ourselves. Nobody thought it was unusual for someone to go to a psychiatrist or even have shock." The problem was that when Eagleton's treatment was exposed to the American public, the general public at large and McGovern specifically were unable to politically explain his psychiatric breakdown. Many people used this incident against him.

On the other hand, some well-educated people are inclined to overlook warning symptoms and stress signals. One friend of mine was getting his degree at Harvard while I was enduring my Calvary at Purdue. His calm, measured attitude and wicked, Noel Coward sense of humor was my mainstay during that long black period. But I was infuriated by the fact that he was so calm and so terribly well adjusted. He was unflappable and always self-assured. The kind of self-assurance that comes from years of line-breeding, Philadelphia Biddles, and fox hunts. Whenever I nattered about my strange dermatological symptoms, he would smirk and lift his left eyebrow in Ivy League disdain. I hated him.

When I had drinks in his proper Ivy League home several years later, I had the courage of a career and a reasonable amount of unravished ego to confess my deep, abiding, bubbling hatred for his calm exterior during that period. His wife hooted in her fox-hunt hoo-hah and said that she would tell me the truth. It seems that my friend, Andrew, was a mass of seething insecurities. A chronic insomniac, he paced the floor at night and meditated on the possible questions that his professors would pose. But his nervousness increased after graduation, and his stress levels grew. And he developed some strange quirks. One of which was that whenever Andrew passed by the window of a typewriter store and saw all those yawning keyboards winking at him, he threw up. After a few of those sessions, his wife convinced him that he really needed some kind of professional therapy. He was lucky he found a good therapist.

Choose with Care

After twelve years of living on the grounds of a psychiatric hospital, I give personal testimony that there are more loons, idiots, nuts, and charlatans alive in the psychotherapeutic community than their patients would ever believe. Beware in-depth therapy. Anybody that wants to keep you for three years or more doesn't know his own business. Watch out for the psychiatrist who has a heavy mortgage, lots of kids, and two or three mistresses. If you walk into a psychiatrist's or psychotherapist's office and the therapist has lipstick on his collar, walk out. One of the raging continual battles among psychiatrists and psychologists is over whether or not it is morally reprehensible to have sex with your patients. Is it perfectly acceptable and good therapy to give these frigid, upset women a little sex on the side?

Some therapists feel that sexual dysfunction, frigidity, corns, bunions, and headaches can be cured by means of sexual relations between therapist and client. Anne Seiden reports that "sexual abuse of the therapeutic relationship is more common and at least sometimes more devastating than has previously been recognized." Phyllis Chesler, in *Women and Madness*, recounts tragic case histories of women whose lives were destroyed and whose mental health was seriously impaired as a result of sexual exploitation by male therapists.

Freud recognized the intimate and erotic nature of psychotherapy, and he warned his disciples that there would always exist the danger of transference on the part of the (female) patient toward the (male) therapist. Granted, some women patients openly seduce the male therapist. However, many male therapists knowingly and cunningly exploit their confused and bewildered women patients. Some therapists have the gall to suggest that sex with the analyst is the best way to "unfreeze" a woman patient's libido. Of such stuff are bordellos and pimps made, not professional ethics.

Always Get a Second Opinion

It's fascinating to realize that most people take better care of their car engines than their heads. Most of us shop around for a good garage mechanic, but we docilely stay with the first shrink, even if the personality clash is obvious from the beginning.

Just as one should seek a second opinion for a mastectomy or a hysterectomy, so also a second opinion for a psychotherapist may be justified. Not maybe, definitely IS. People in the United States and women in particular unfortunately incline toward treating doctors as the Great God Mammon. Anybody who can use a stethoscope or write a prescription obviously has to be inviolable. The same thing goes for therapists. Whether M.D., Ph.D., psychologist, M.A., social worker, or the pentecostal minister down the street—not everybody is qualified to help others with emotional problems. Terry is a case in point.

Terry and the Pirate

One evening while I was living on the grounds of the psychiatric hospital, my friend Terry called me up. She was incensed at one doctor while blessing another. Terry and I had been graduate students together, although her stress was further exacerbated by two teen-age daughters and a traveling-salesman husband. After a long, glum, dreary, sunless Indiana winter, she finally went to Dr. Townly.

Terry told him about her graduate-student paranoia, her teen-ager's rebellion, her loneliness, and her mediocre sex life. Townly leaned across the table and said to her, "You're suicidal. You have to be hospitalized immediately."

Terry replied, "But, my God, I have two girls at home alone and I can't go to the hospital right now."

Townly argued, "I am the doctor! I know what is wrong with you! You are suicidal, you have to be hospitalized; you are one of the worst cases I have ever seen!"

Somehow Terry was able to hold herself together, promise Dr. Townly that she would take a cab out to the local hospital, sign herself in, and begin in-depth therapy immediately. Even though she was in a terrifically excited state, she knew that it was immediately necessary to make some kind of arrangements for her teen-age daughters. On arriving home, by chance and God's grace, the husband had returned from his trip and was sitting in the living room. A man of inordinate good sense, once he had heard Terry's agitated story he simply said, "We need a second opinion." He then called another psychiatrist in town, an extremely conservative doctor. They made an appointment immediately with Dr. Kirk, who stayed in his office in order to talk to Terry and her husband.

During this interview, Kirk was the exact antithesis of Townly. Kirk leaned back in his chair and proceeded to tell Terry that she was no more suicidal than he. Kirk admitted that he, too, had suffered from a long winter, and his problems concerned three, not two, teen-age daughters. Kirk, of course, refused to malign his fellow psychiatrist, Townly, but assured Terry that neither tranquilizers, sleeping pills, in-depth therapy, nor hospitalization were in order. He did prescribe a change of scene, perhaps a weekend away or, better yet, sending the girls away to visit their grandmother —but that was all.

Those were other days and other times. Perhaps today Terry would sue Dr. Townly. But those were the days when we believed doctors were almost infallible. Luckily, Terry found Kirk at an extremely important time in her life. But the lesson to be learned from Terry is definitely, surely, always, and without doubt, get the second opinion. You would get a second opinion if you had to go into an operation. Wouldn't you? Unfortunately, most of us would not. The statistics, for example, show that when women get a second opinion whether or not they should have a hysterectomy, *at least one half* of the doctors state that the hysterectomy is not necessary. What kind of a second opinion would you get with psychotherapy? More likely than not, it would depend upon the personal bent of the therapist.

My Therapy Is Better Than Your Therapy

Just as there are fashions in clothes, so also are there fads and fancies in psychotherapy. Freudian analysis, transactional analysis, encounter groups, primal scream, reality therapy, etc. One thing to remember about therapy is that when we divide one hundred psychiatric patients into fifty getting therapy of some type and fifty not, in each group twenty-five will get well. That indicates that the success rate of those who get therapy and those who don't is equal. Given these statistics, probably the best thing to do is not to get therapy at all.

However, the therapeutic situation is a psychiatric and

support prop that we all desperately need. In a highly mobile society like the United States, where one out of every five families move at least once a year, the average time between moves is 3.6 years. Mama lives in Chicago and daughter lives in California. Often, our priest, minister, or best friend is absent. One reason for the success of Dr. Spock is that young mothers turn to Spock for advice because they cannot turn to their own mother. So "experts" step in where the family fails.

In other cultures, the expert can be a shaman or medicine man. For example, Navajo medicine men, or chicano *curanderos*, have just as much success with psychotic patients as therapists in large state hospitals. Perhaps even more. Whether it is Zen Buddhism, Arica, I'm okay you're okay, or the host of do-it-yourself books available in your local drugstore, advice proliferates to help us cope.

Primal Scream—Forest Primeval

One of the fads of the 1960s was "primal scream." The idea behind this fad was that if you were oversocialized and had a thick veneer built up, you could never learn to express inner hostility. So you were encouraged to scream and scream and scream and pound pillows and hit big plastic dummies and scream and scream. . . .

It wasn't very good for the vocal cords and often did little more than relieve tension. Perhaps there was some grain of truth in the idea that many people are unable—emotionally or psychologically—to express their anger. The screaming was an attempt to release that anger. But usually it was no more than yelling.

One psychiatric hospital administrator found little use for primal scream. One of the psychotherapists in the hospital had become enamored of primal-scream therapy and had moved all the furniture out of his office save for pillows, mats, the punching-bag plastic dummy, and a few boxes of Kleenex. This outré office was just down the hall from the administrator, who was in the midst of a high-pressure fund-raising campaign. One afternoon, as Carl, the administrator, was explaining to a prospective donor about the new look in psychiatry, he found himself in the midst of a comic Greek chorus.

"You know that we no longer lock people up in dark, dank wards with straitjackets," explained Carl.

"YEAAAAAHHHHHHHH," a voice howled down the hall.

"Psychiatry is a respectable branch of medicine, and our staff are some of the finest and best-trained in the whole country," Carl valiantly continued.

"Scream! YELL! LET IT ALL HANG OUT!!!," thundered a new voice in the office down the way.

Sounds of thumping and pounding came into the administrator's office, in combination with sobs, sighs, and assorted screams and moans.

Carl gave up. He leapt out of his chair and ran down the hall. He broke into Dr. Fagel's primal-scream session and picked up Fagel like a terrier shaking a rat.

"Listen here, you S.O.B.," Carl snapped, "if I ever catch you playing these silly games in this office when I have a hot prospect in mine, I'll kill you."

Dr. Fagel understood the message and was well aware of Carl's inner hostility. As a matter of fact, Carl expressed his inner feelings and his deep-seated hostility in a most effective manner. I never did find out what happened to Fagel's patient. All I know is that Fagel took up the mattresses and moved out of primal-scream therapy.

If screaming doesn't seem to be your particular bent, there are other therapists willing to cure your ills by whatever bizarre means possible. Vegetarian diets. High-protein powders. If you read *Reader's Digest* long enough, you can find any mental illness or stress-related disease and its attendant cure. The "in" disease of the mid seventies was hypoglycemia. It was rather cute to have and was nontransmittable. Its cure? A high-protein diet, fresh air, and lots of exercise.

Chic illnesses aside, women are more prone to depression than are men. There are at least two women diagnosed as depressive compared to every man. Other studies report a ratio of three women depressives to every male so diagnosed. Depression is an acceptable way for females to show their distress. Some of the symptoms are listlessness, withdrawal, apathetic behavior, and extreme dependency. In other words, as Chesler points out, depressive behavior is "exaggerated female behavior." Treating depression with mood-altering drugs is counterproductive and actually dangerous.

Depression is chic this year too. As we focus more attention on depression, we have to analyze those sex-role behaviors that encourage depressive behavior. *Long Day's Journey into Night* is still being replayed in the living rooms of suburbia. There has to be some way out of the depression trap.

Women Therapists

One way is to seek out a female therapist. There are raging arguments within and without the helping professions concerning whether a member of an "in-group" is the best kind of therapist. Some people say that only an insider, a person who has suffered the same deprivations and experiences as the client, can build a bond of empathy. Reformed alcoholics who know the wretched craving for liquor help alcoholics in Alcoholics Anonymous. Former junkies help addicts in Synanon. Weight Watchers lecturers are former fatties. There is some logic to the insider argument.

There is a decided fallacy as well. Not all women are nice. Not all women therapists are competent. Not all male therapists are exploitative nincompoops. Yet the advantage of women therapists seems to be that there is a high likelihood that they will have experienced similar problems. One of the most touching scenes in the movie *An Unmarried Woman* is where the heroine breaks down in therapy over the prospect of living a life divorced and alone. The woman psychotherapist then begins her account of *her* problems in readjustment after a divorce. That's empathy. Women seem to erase the superior/inferior client/patient role and actively work *together* to find solutions to the patient's problems.

Women's Groups

If one-to-one therapy is too expensive, women's groups may provide the kind of support system that you need.

Remember that a person alone is prone to physical and emotional stress. Support systems are necessary elements for good mental health. Many authors have written extensively on the concept of male bonding and forget that there is a heavy emphasis in all societies on female bonding. Female bonding may be organized needle-point clubs, the League of Women Voters, the P.T.A., or a neighborhood *Kaffeeklatsch*. Mothers meeting in a park with bouncing babies in prams are manifestations of female bonding systems. Whatever the extent of these contacts, they usually prove to give some meaning to many women's lives.

In spite of some drubbings in the press and mutterings from a few unhappy husbands, women's consciousness-raising groups have changed many women's lives. For ill and for good. Some of these groups grew out of local YWCAs or church groups, were adjuncts to women's professional organizations, or were just neighborhood women gathering together. Using little or no structure, the women's group provided a means by which women could share their problems and misgivings with other women. Some women found out that their marital relationships were shabby at best and enslavement at worst. Other women realized that wife beating is a sick pattern and that they no longer had to endure such abuse. Women's groups gave support and advice to women going through divorce or re-entering the job market.

In my own case, women's groups provided me with encouraging peer and political clout. Women sociologists gathered together in the Women's Caucus and later in the organization known as Sociologists for Women in Society.

Learning and maneuvering in a smaller arena, many women sociologists were encouraged by their success to write books, run for office within the American Sociological Association, seek high-ranking jobs, and generally behave like aggressive male professionals. In the Latin American Studies Association, women formed an interdisciplinary alliance and elected board members, vice-presidents, program chairpeople, and finally a president—in a predominantly male organization. Most of the women in these two organizations received accolades from their women colleagues, and the resulting increased security helped impel them to greater success.

Help is available. Many women's problems are reality-based: Not enough money. Adolescent rebellion. Alcoholism. Wife beating. Child abuse. Every suburban neighborhood can match the ghetto with family horror stories. But there are ways out. The question is whether you take them or sink even further into depression.

10

Stress and the Ultimate Solution: Suicide

THIS is not a nice chapter. As a matter of fact, it is an acutely depressing chapter. So if you have contemplated suicide, attempted suicide, are thinking now of suicide, or in any way have thought processes associated with suicide, you ought not to read this chapter. However, on second thought, given that perhaps you or your friends, spouse, or relatives may be in this state, this chapter *might* possibly help you in some way. But be forewarned: the ultimate stress reaction is not a pleasant subject.

Suicide Statistics

And so first to some depressing statistics. Suicide is primarily a male phenomenon. More men commit suicide than women. Men use guns or knives or hang themselves. More women attempt or threaten suicide than do men. Women kill themselves without maiming their bodies. Women are more likely than men to turn on the gas or use pills to end it all. Although world-wide statistics indicate that more men can get the job done in a faster and more grisly manner, female suicides are on the increase. In the United States, suicide is the tenth-leading cause of death in the country. Once every minute of every day, someone in the United States tries to kill himself, and once every twenty-four minutes, someone succeeds. Over twenty thousand persons kill themselves every year. While male-female ratios are changing, there are other important variables that impinge on suicide statistics. Older men and women are much more likely to commit suicide than younger people. However, in the United States young adolescents are killing themselves at faster rates. In the fifteen-to-nineteen-year-old group, for example, suicide is the third-ranking cause of death, exceeded only by accident and cancer. Besides, how many of those automobile accidents are really suicide? Also, single, divorced, and widowed persons are more likely than married people to kill themselves. Once again, we see that statistics are intertwined with reality, because the older you are the more likely you are to be divorced or widowed. Nonetheless, older, widowed men are more likely to kill themselves than older, widowed women. Perhaps what is most frightening of all is the propensity for young adolescents and even children to fall prey to depressive states and end their lives.

Variations on a Theme

Like most statistical profiles, the figures on suicide are extremely clouded. The National Center for Health Statistics does not separate male/female statistics by whether or not the person is employed. Thus we have no idea whether or not working women kill themselves at a higher rate than housewives. However, more and more women are entering the labor force. For example, in 1940, women constituted 27 per cent of the labor force; in 1960, the proportion of women workers had risen to 36 per cent; and by 1971, 43 per cent of workers were women. Also by 1971, 63 per cent of the working women were married and nearly 40 per cent of working women were mothers of children under eight-

Suicide Rates by Color and Sex 1950–76
(per 100,000 population)

YEAR	WHITE MALES	WHITE FEMALES	ALL OTHER MALES	ALL OTHER FEMALES
1950	18.1	5.3	7.8	1.8
1955	16.5	4.8	7.1	1.7
1960	17.5	5.3	8.7	2.3
1965	17.7	6.7	9.7	3.0
1970	18.0	7.1	8.5	2.9
1975	20.1	7.4	10.6	3.3
1976	19.8	7.2	11.0	3.2

Source: National Center for Health Statistics, U.S. Department of Health, Education, and Welfare, Washington, D.C.

een years of age. Since 1950, suicide rates have risen slowly for men and somewhat more quickly for women. Suicide rates have jumped dramatically for non-white males and females since 1950. Thus there is probably some link between women entering the labor force and increasing rates of suicide.

There is variation by profession. Of all professionals, doctors are most prone to commit suicide. Male doctors commit suicide at a rate twice that for all males in the population as a whole. More doctors die as a result of suicide than from plane crashes, drownings, or homicide. The number of doctors—men and women—who commit suicide every year nearly equals the number of graduates from one average graduating medical-school class. And of all physicians, psychiatrists commit suicide more than three times the normal rate for the society as a whole. Even more surprising is the finding that women doctors and women medical students commit suicide at a rate *four times* the rate for women in the United States. The woman doctor or woman medical student is far more likely to be unmarried than her male-physician-suicide counterpart. But male physicians are more likely to commit suicide after age forty-five, while women doctors kill themselves before age forty-five.

While most research on women professionals has concentrated on the woman medical student or woman physician, there are a few studies that indicate that female professionals in other fields are prone to suicide also. Women psychologists kill themselves at a rate three times that of the population as a whole. While women constitute a minuscule percentage of members of the American Chemical

Society, women are 11 per cent of the suicides. Even though these studies perhaps err on the side of caution, since suicide is often underreported or deliberately hidden by police and close family relatives, the implication is chilling. Yet classical sociological theory has an explanation for high suicide rates among women professionals.

At the turn of the century, Durkheim analyzed suicide. He concluded that there was a kind of suicide as the result of *anomie*. The anomic suicide is a person who takes his or her own life because there are not enough norms, supporting relationships, ties, responsibilities, or links to the community as a whole. Thus the lonely, the old, the unmarried, and the childless are the most likely to kill themselves. Lack of roots, feelings of loss, lack of meaning in life, and sense of purposelessness are all factors in anomie. Thus, we can see why a sole woman professional or one woman out of a scant two or three women in a medical-school class or the single woman resident in a large city hospital would feel harassed and overly pressured. Also, young women suffer from societal and cultural pressure to marry and have children while fulfilling or even over-fulfilling their professional obligations. No wonder, then, that talented, harried, worried, frustrated young women become so frustrated and depressed that they kill themselves. With few peers and even fewer role models (i.e., older women doctors who have combined marriage and success and children), they do not just *feel* alone, they *are* alone.

However, these depressing statistics should decrease in future years. As the number of women in professions (particularly medicine) increases, the suicide rate for women should drop. Currently, women constitute 6 per cent of the medical profession; however, 20–24 per cent of medical students are women. Thus, as more and more women enter medicine and the peer support from other women widens and the number of women role models increases, loneliness and anguish must decrease. This prediction is borne out by the lack of depression and the high coping skills of women professionals in Argentina. Peer support, role models, cultural acceptance of women in a "male" profession, and female role models all lessen anomie. The less anomie, the less depression.

Depression

Depression is the most important link in suicide. Loneliness, feelings of being useless, a meaningless life, fear of illness—whatever the perceived or real reason, suicide is one way to solve an insoluble problem. No pain. No sorrow. No loneliness. No worries. Only the void and the beyond. A terror that some of us are unable to comprehend. Perhaps it is indeed not the coward's way, but that of the brave, who determine their own fate.

Never believe the folk wisdom concerning this very determined desire. Common-sense folklore tells you that a person who threatens suicide is the very person who will *not* commit suicide. Wrong! People who talk of suicide or threaten to kill themselves are sending out messages calling for help. This threat, this call for help, often goes unanswered, because it is too often repeated. The woman who says that she will kill herself if her husband leaves her may kill herself if her husband stays with her. There are signs and portents all the way, which the family, only after the deed is done, can reconstruct and re-examine. If nothing else, a radical change in behavior is but one forewarning.

Depression is easy to spot. A woman becomes dull, slovenly, unkempt, and uninterested in anything. Her personal appearance begins to deteriorate. She stops going to the hairdresser, slops around the house in a dirty dress or housecoat, her stockings with runs in them. She is not too clean and neither is her house. The dirty dishes overrun the sink, and her home disintegrates into a pigsty. She refuses to go out. She won't have friends in. Her only entertainment may be the flickering tube. She doesn't read, refuses to answer the telephone. Slowly and effectively, she cuts herself off from life. The husband or friends can't seem to talk any sense to her. Attempts at therapy fail. Then she begins a magical transformation. She may join a church or seek therapy or join a few clubs. She goes to the hairdresser. She makes a valiant attempt to improve her appearance, and the house sparkles. This is what the therapists call a state of "agitated depression." She seeks some sort of meaning and order in her life. She straightens up her stockings, her dresser drawers, her bank accounts, and some missing threads in her life. Anita was such a case history.

Anita—Classic Housewife Victim

Anita could be diagnosed as a depressed housewife who exhibited the "empty-nest syndrome." Menopause, children leaving home, and a workaholic husband were combination enough to contribute to Anita's depression. Even her well-meaning but self-absorbed husband saw the drastic changes in his once orderly home and his formerly well-groomed Anita. He persuaded Anita to talk to the family minister, who, in turn, got Anita to visit the local mental-health clinic. While she was hesitant about joining group therapy, she acceded to her psychotherapist's wishes. Soon the therapy sessions became all-absorbing. She eagerly looked forward to Wednesday nights and came home anxious to share her insights with her husband, Arthur. Arthur, too, was pleased with Anita's progress, but he was unable to enter into her interminable discussions of why she had gone wrong and where he had failed and what they both had to do in order to revitalize their marriage.

Anita tried time and time again to persuade Arthur to go with her to the therapist, sit in on the group-therapy sessions, or seek other kinds of counsel. Arthur refused to admit that he had any influence or bearing on Anita's behavior. Besides, he felt that Anita was "going through the change" and would somehow snap out of everything. She snapped, all right. Like many agitated depressives, she cleaned up the house, went to the hairdresser, bought a new dress, returned home, wrote a note, and swallowed the bottle of pills. She made no fuss and definitely no muss. The police found her on top of the bed, with nary a wrinkle on the bedspread. Like the nice, middle-class Wasp lady that she was, she didn't cause a stir or a ripple.

Intent—Reality or Fantasy

Sometimes the family isn't so lucky. When the lady of the household does herself in, sometimes she takes others along with her. One case that hit the papers a few years ago shows how plans can go astray. A nice, middle-class Caucasian lady in a nice, hundred-thousand-dollar home got up early one morning, went to the closed garage, and turned on the motor of her Bentley. Unfortunately for her two sons and husband, the carbon monoxide seeped into the house, and the car-pool driver found four dead bodies instead of the single suicide intended.

Actually, intent is sometimes hard to determine. Maybe this woman really meant to do a grisly opera finale, but who will ever know? Certainly, more women attempt suicide than actually commit it. This means that many of those who end up dead didn't really mean to at all. The Marilyn Monroe syndrome, of calling up friends, peers, relatives, or your poor, harassed psychiatrist, and threatening suicide, is a case in point. I have been victimized by wild friends calling in the middle of the night and muttering their dire threats over the telephone. In the dead of winter, I have changed my nightgown for street clothes and slid over icy streets to save my desperate friend. On arriving in the wee hours of the morning and pounding on apartment doors, I have been greeted by steamy cups of coffee, tears, and incoherent babbling. Enough of rescuers. Enough of saving lives. I empathized with Marilyn Monroe's tired and embittered psychiatrist, who told her to turn over and go back to sleep. How many times had he gone riding to the rescue? How many nights had he had to put up with babysitting a millionaire movie star? Apparently, too many nights and too many times. Patience wears thin and there seems no way to break through the layers and layers of indifference and parasitic demands.

Sally—the Good and Bad Nurse

That's what happened to Sally, a wise psychiatric nurse, who has a tale that she tells on herself after two martinis and much prodding. Her story shows how exasperation and fatigue produced the wonder cure for a depressed suicide.

When Sally was much much younger and much less wise, she was on a one-to-one watch with an agitated, suicidal woman patient. Sally had just resigned her job, was accepted into graduate school, and knew that she had brilliant career prospects with a rich, full life after her navy experience. Her last assignment in the hospital was to watch over a suicidal navy dependent wife (Nancy). In two weeks Sally was off to vacation and then her master's degree. Sally was as worried and as desperate as the patient. They skirted around each other like prizefighters. Nancy tried to jam her toothbrush down her throat, and Sally fought that attempt. Nancy's doctor wanted to avoid heavy sedation, so Nancy and Sally wrestled night after night, tore bedsheets apart, banged closet doors, and Nancy banged her head repeatedly on the wall. Nancy was in light restraints, then in heavy restraints; had light tranquilizers; had cold baths, warm showers, and whatever else the doctor thought would calm poor, demented Nancy down.

Night after night, Sally begged Nancy, "Kill yourself. Please, dear God, kill yourself. But for all that is holy and for whatever it is worth, please, for the love of heaven, don't kill yourself on *my* watch." She kept telling Nancy, "I don't care if you kill yourself. I don't give a damn if you kill yourself. But if you die now, I won't go to graduate school. I'll never get out of here. You just don't understand them. I'll never get a good recommendation. Listen, just listen to me! Wait until tomorrow afternoon and kill yourself, with that awful head nurse on duty. They won't touch her. But please don't get me in trouble."

Obviously this was the worst possible type of therapy and the worst type of psychiatry possible. Nancy stared balefully at Sally. Sometimes Nancy would growl or mutter curses at Sally as she rocked back and forth on the bed ready to spring at Sally and scratch her eyes out. Night after night, the mutterings, moanings, beggings, pleadings, and curses continued.

Nancy got well. Sally can tell the story, because her mismanagement of the case, combined with her superbly inappropriate behavior, resulted in her becoming the one lucid hateful object in Nancy's life. I know Nancy, and her version is that she became so angry at Sally for begging her to kill herself that she decided that, no matter what, she would get better only for one purpose: She was going to fake out the doctors, get released from restraints and the close, one-to-one suicide watch, and kill herself on Sally's shift in order to ruin Sally for life. The plan went awry, because Nancy's will to improve meant that as she regained her sanity she saw the stupidity of the whole suicide gesture. So all the non-efficient and bad nursing precepts had a salutary effect, because Nancy got better and Sally received a commendation for her superior nursing. As the result of Sally's short temper, death was cheated.

Lena and the Pills

Cases like Nancy's have a certain wry humor, and humor is hard to come by in the tragedy of suicide. Lena's story is so typical and so stupid.

Lena had several stressful events occur all at once: One month after her beloved mother died of cancer, her father had a serious heart attack. While Lena was flying back and forth from her home to her father's bedside, Lena's little girl broke her leg in a silly playground accident. Also, her husband was working too hard to become a plant manager. Lena had had a nice job in a boutique in the local shopping center. She explained rather ruefully, "It wasn't much, but it was all I had. It meant a great deal to me."

Lena had to quit her job because of her myriad family problems, and she went to her family physician for a few tranquilizers to help her through this particularly painful period; then she felt much better, during the day.

She began to have problems sleeping. So the doctor prescribed sleeping pills. Then Lena began to have problems waking up. The vicious cycle had begun. Pills to go to sleep, pills to get up in the morning, pills to keep going through the afternoon, and then the pills to go to sleep.

She had problems making decisions, and her life was rather blurred. Nevertheless she could make it through the day without crying or screaming at her little girl. Sex had never interested her, and now with the sleeping pills she was never awake enough to respond to her husband. The weeks and months slipped by. Her father improved and the little girl's cast came off. The problems of the moment were gone and Lena kept right on taking her pills. She was hooked. Everything came to a screeching halt when she drove out of Sears' parking lot and smashed broadside into a car. Of course it was Lena's fault.

Luckily no one was seriously hurt. Lena and her daughter were bruised. Lena's car was totaled and the insurance company declared her a bad risk. Moreover, Lena's husband declared her a bad risk and put her into a mental hospital to go off the pills. With reasonably good psychiatric care and a long tapering-off period, she shook her daily pills-to-get-up-pills-to-go-to-sleep routine. However, when she returned home the walls started to close in on her. Lena's obsessive-compulsive housecleaning behavior began. Everything had to be spic and span, clean, neat, tidied up just as in *House Beautiful*. Cleaning, scrubbing, washing, raking, painting, wallpapering, Lena became maniacal over her home. Once again she sought a physician's help. This time it was a new doctor, because the GP wouldn't give her any more prescriptions. She innocently asked her gynecologist for something to help her sleep. He willingly became her accomplice. Then the dermatologist wrote a prescription for uppers and became part of Lena's conspiracy. The only problem was that Lena's conspiracy was directed by her against herself.

Lena's husband searched the medicine cabinets and drawers but never found the pills. Junkies and boozers have unique hiding places and you can look for a thousand years and never find the bottle in the trash bin or pills stuffed in the toes of evening slippers. Lena's husband ranted and threatened, but Lena kept on. But one day the pills didn't help her depression enough. She went into the bathroom and calmly and efficiently cut her wrists.

Apparently she didn't mean to complete her suicide, because she walked into the kitchen holding her wrists in the air and frightened her little girl out of her wits. The husband quickly put a tourniquet on Lena's wrists and called the ambulance. While Lena was waiting to be carted off to the hospital again, she told her husband that he ought to use cold water to remove the bloodstains she had left on the living-room broadloom as she crossed from the bathroom to the kitchen. Then the husband came to the awful realization that Lena was crazy as a loon and always would be crazy. Suicide, cold water for the bloodstains, clean toilet bowls, a father's heart attack, and complete disregard for the daughter were all intertwined. That was the moment of truth, when he decided to put Lena in the state hospital, get a no-fault divorce, sell the house, arrange for a job transfer, take his little girl, and get the hell out. When Lena got off the pills and found out that she was truly abandoned, she hanged herself from the bars in the hospital's recreation room.

Anyone's death leaves a void, however small. Friends, relatives, newspaper readers, hard-bitten policemen, or whoever, can be and are deeply affected by one person's willfully taking her life into her own hands. To wantonly, carefully, carelessly, or calculatingly choose the moment of one's death is frightening. Becoming the true determiner of one's own fate is awesome.

But suicide is not only and always born of despair but

often meant to lash out at and "pay back" friends or relatives. It is the ultimate in the unholy game of I'll-get-you-back-because-you-were-mean-to-me. If-you-hurt-me,-I'll-kill-myself-and-burden-you-with-guilt-forever-and-ever. In a weird and wild rationale, this suicide hopes that by killing herself—or even just attempting to kill herself—she can bind a loved one closer and closer with ties of guilt/shame or honor. What Durkheim called "egoistic suicide," or the "get-even suicide," is probably more prevalent among women than men.

Doris and the Guilt Trip

Doris is a fairly straightforward suicide note on a police blotter. She had no previous history of mental illness, but friends and neighbors reported that she was "fairly highstrung" and used to yell at her husband and children a great deal. Doris' mother had committed suicide, however, and that is often a flag for therapists. We all learn by example and role models. So if one member of your family committed suicide, that's one example for you to use when searching for methods in which to solve your problems. Doris' problems were not insurmountable, but they were *her* problems and for *her* were indeed insurmountable.

Doris' kids were neither the brightest nor the best. Her husband regularly disappeared, only to return with lipstick on his collar. While he denied swift, casual affairs, the evidence was overwhelming. Finally he asked Doris for a divorce, and her world crumbled around her. She begged, pleaded, cried, threw tantrums, and he still wanted a divorce. Doris finally persuaded him to enter therapy with her and try to solve their marital difficulties. Marriage therapists are well aware that when a couple is hell bent for the divorce court no amount of therapy can help an unwilling spouse. It also doesn't help when there is a third party waiting eagerly in the wings for a soon-to-be-released spouse. So Harold, the husband, left, and Doris had to find a divorce lawyer in a hurry if she was to get any alimony or child support.

Days of wrangling with Harold and his lawyers and nights of trying to cope with her rambunctious and very confused brood left her drained both physically and psychologically. She didn't eat or sleep and lost weight at an alarming rate. Doris found out where Harold and his girlfriend were living, and she would haunt the apartment parking lot, hoping to catch him for a few moments and try to persuade him to return home. Harold was delighted that he had a new, nubile, and bouncy girlfriend and his once shrewish wife was now abjectly begging him to return.

The scenario played on and on, with lonely nights and tension-filled days. Doris called Harold at the office until his secretary was told never to accept any more calls. Harold had to have an unlisted number to avoid Doris' continual calls. Doris adopted a ploy then of sending telegrams to Harold's apartment saying that one of the children was in the hospital emergency ward or that she had had an accident. Doris used any trick or lie she could think of only to have Harold come rushing over. Once Harold had played a few of these "wolf-wolf" games, he stopped rushing over and sometimes would send the police instead. Both Harold and his girlfriend were getting fed up with

Doris' wild rantings and the police got to the point that they would attempt to soothe Doris over the telephone, refusing to relay her messages. So when Doris became aware that her scare tactics were not working, she decided on a more dramatic play. She probably had lost control and was despondent, confused, and desperately alone. But these are only guesses. She might actually have rationally calculated that Harold was a decent man who would be appalled at the extreme depths to which he had driven his once-beloved wife. Maybe she didn't mean to kill herself but only meant to scare Harold and make him come back home.

We will never know, because Doris became an over-thirty-five, divorced, female statistic. When one of the daughters returned home from high school, she found her mother in the car in the closed garage. Death by carbon-monoxide poisoning was the verdict. Death by a broken heart is what Harold thinks. Maybe it is death by accident. Doris was a creature of habit. Nearly every day, she waited for one of her neighbors, who worked part time, to come home precisely at three-thirty o'clock and the two of them would have coffee together. Lately, however, the neighbor had not been returning home, precisely because Doris' whining complaints were both boring and depressing. So the neighbor invented trips to the grocery store or the hairdresser to avoid meeting Doris. The coroner said that Doris had died sometime around four o'clock. Perhaps the neighbor was supposed to have played her part in Doris' suicide rehearsal by stopping her from entering the garage or miraculously hearing the car start up in the closed but unlocked garage. The neighbor was to have then called police, rescue squad, ministers, daughters, and, of course, Harold. When the police did finally tell Harold, he was upset but not as upset and guilty as the neighbor, who never quite forgave herself for coming home too late to save poor Doris.

When Is It Suicide?

There are lots of poor Dorises in this world. In fact, there are lots of poor Harolds in this world as well. We could continue this unhappy litany of more and more grisly suicide cases and never come to any conclusions surrounding these tales of complete misery. However, some of the stories, like Doris', raise many questions.

Even though we know that suicide is the second-most-frequent cause of death among young people—next only to automobile accidents—our data on suicide are (and probably always will be) incomplete.

Is it suicide when a young woman drives off a hill on a dry highway on a sunny day? Is it suicide when another takes a curve too fast on a slick highway on a rainy day? And what about smoking? Some people contend that those who smoke to excess are themselves committing suicide. You can read the warnings on the packages. You know what your doctors say to you. You know what your lungs feel like with that constant reaching for a cigarette. The constant reaching for a cigarette may be itself a suicidal gesture. In fact, the workaholic male and the workaholic female are also not paying any attention to the warning signs of stress.

The Workaholic

The workaholic is the one that you have to watch, because he or she is always so tricky. The workaholic contends that he or she is working for the good of the family, the good of the company, the good of the profession—all the random excuses that don't really tell you what the workaholic is doing. Workaholics, like alcoholics, are escape artists. Escapists, that is.

Work can be a joy. Work can be an escape. The workaholic is running away from friends, family, obligations, or emotional involvement. Workaholics know that, like drugs, alcohol, and sex, work can be thrilling, a constant high. The fun thing about work is that people don't blame you, in our society, for working.

Here's where women fall into the male trap. Women who are entering the corporation board rooms, executive councils, directorates, and managerial cadre may be workaholics just as much as men have had to be. Women often are convinced of the old saw that a professional woman "has to think like a man, act like a lady, and work like a dog." I don't even think that the oft-quoted proverb is funny or even worth quoting, but many women are adopting those male standards of aggression, pushiness, hard work, and suicidal dedication that we all consider necessary for realizing the American dream. As a result, women are also denying themselves those pleasures and those joys in life that men have denied themselves for, lo, these many years. The sweet smell of success is played off against Manhattan tower offices, rosewood paneling, broadloom on the floor, too many cigarettes, a lot of coffee, shaking hands, and shooting pains down the arm.

Remember, this is a blanket condemnation of the workaholic—irrespective of sex. All work and no play makes Jack and Jill not only dull but essentially nasty people. The driven personality will usually drive his or her staff—eventually driving them out of the office to another firm. Yet, we know that presidents of large corporations are less inclined to coronaries than are the *vice*-presidents. Success reaps its own rewards, and good health seems to be one of them. Also, in the chapter on management styles, we showed how the new participatory-nurturant management styles are consistent with traditional female socialization. So maybe the ulcer-prone and/or ulcer-giving female manager is an anomaly. Like Hallie.

Hallie the Corporation Vice-President

Hallie is a nice southern lady. She has wit, charm, verve, excitement, education, and a lot of energy. Hallie is a fast-rising executive, now vice-president of a large publishing company in New York. She keeps her figure trim, wears beautiful three-piece executive-sharkskin suits with Givenchy blouses and Dior scarves. Hallie also works twelve hours a day. She doesn't eat properly. Gets very little sleep. And lately her skin is blotchy and her hair is falling out. Hallie doesn't understand why. Hallie really does know what is wrong. She knows that in her unremitting, unrelenting rise to the top she is paying the price in psychological and physiological stress. Those twelve-hour days can extend into twenty hours, because Hallie lugs work back home. When Hallie takes business trips, she works in the airport lounge and travels first class so she can spread her papers out and arrive on top of whatever situation will greet her in the next city. One time last year, during a bout with the flu, Hallie was delighted to be able to have an excuse to stay at home. Being so sick that she could not go to the office meant that Hallie could prop herself up in bed and write a twenty-page professional paper that was presented at a professional meeting and also now is to be published in a management journal. Hallie is a reasonably adjusted young woman, and she knows that the price of receiving all the riches of this earth may indeed be too high.

Her friends, her doctors, and even casual acquaintances have told Hallie to slow down; stop being the Sammy Glick of the New York publishing business. So, on those often all-too-infrequent evenings when Hallie has time, she plays almost as hard as she works. Frantic discothèque dancing, catching up on art and theater, in a tremendous, mad kind of rush. Hallie has to be the on-stage, with-it-generation female that is the delight of the women's magazines.

There really is no prognosis for Hallie at this point. I cite her case as an example of some of the things that perhaps ought to be avoided. All the signs of stress are there, but Hallie is ignoring them. The next time around, it will take not just a case of influenza but a full-blown high-blood-pressure-and-ringing-in-the-ears attack to make Hallie slow down. No, technically, Hallie is not suicidal. Hallie is only killing herself through her work. The epitaph may read, "She drove herself to death."

The Long-term Prognosis for Everybody

While workaholics like Hallie can be considered somewhat suicidal, the statistics do not include them. Suicides include pill poppers, alcoholics, and those who use knives, guns, gas, and the myriad other methods to end their lives. The long-term outlook seems to be worse and worse. More people are killing themselves at a faster rate; young people, old people. This is the price that we all seem to be paying, one way or the other.

This is a desperate and depressing chapter. The facts of death are depressing indeed. Is there no way that we can reduce the number of Dorises, Hallies, and Lenas? Perhaps there are ways.

For one thing, women should become familiar with the depressing statistics and warning signals of suicide. We continually hear about the seven warning signs of cancer. Why not publicize the warning signs of suicide? Death is a taboo topic in our society, and we don't like to discuss, learn about, or meditate on suicide or death. Even the simple and intelligent act of making a will is regarded by many people as a portent of imminent death. We should recognize depression, alcoholism, drug addiction, and even overwork as potential time bombs leading to suicide or accidental death.

Durkheim's analysis of anomic suicide has practical application. Realizing that those persons with the least amount of peer, friend, kin, or marital support networks are those people most likely to commit suicide, cities and towns throughout the United States have set up suicide "hot lines." Even in those instances in which a person has made a decision to take his or her life, there is the possibility of rescue via the telephone. Suicide hot-line rescues make good television half-hour dramas, but they also work. Lonely, frightened, distraught people, men and women with suicide intentions, still make feeble attempts to link themselves with the community at large and survive.

Thus, no matter how trivial a gesture or how feeble an effort, we must try to stretch out the hand of friendship to those people we know are lonely. Or if we suffer from loneliness ourselves, we must make the gigantic effort to surmount the loneliness. What can be done?

Well, the first thing to remember is that all holidays are depressing. After watching television presentations of Tiny Tim or *Miracle on 34th Street* or Bing Crosby in *White Christmas* or a Christmas gathering of your favorite soap-opera characters, you can get depressed enough to blow your brains out if you don't have close family kin to celebrate a Happy and Merry Christmas. I am living proof, by the way, of the non-anomic possibilities of Christmas. Usually every Christmas I am more homicidal than suicidal. I cook, clean, wrap presents, prepare gourmet dishes for children who exclaim "YUCCKK," set an elegant table for some avid football fans who can't tear themselves away from the television set, and then wonder why I greet the holidays with clenched teeth. Alone is worse.

So if you live alone, find yourself a group of equally lonely waifs who have family away, are recently divorced, or are simply strangers in town. I have had some incredibly pleasant Christmases and Easters with my own collections of orphans of the storm. Even if the dinner is a colossal failure, it does stave off loneliness. One Thanksgiving, in Argentina, I decided to chase away my Thanksgiving depression by cooking an elegant and very typical Thanksgiving dinner for my Argentine friends. I searched the city for a fat turkey and found a somewhat scrawny bird that bore no resemblance to the plump Butterball birds from the U.S. Safeway. I conned a PanAm stewardess into bringing two cans of pumpkin and one can of cranberry sauce from the States. I cooked, cleaned, hummed, made my pumpkin pies, and stuffed and roasted my skinny turkey. My Argentine guests were enthralled with sharing an American national holiday with me. But they were used to eating turkey cold. Never eat turkey hot. One person exclaimed, "In Argentina, we only serve pumpkin to pigs. You mean in the United States people actually eat this stuff!" Everyone pushed the cranberry sauce around their plates and said it was "interesting." I cried over my Argentine Thanksgiving. But they were tears of rage and not loneliness. Maybe that is mental healthiness of one sort or the other.

Aside from cooking and arranging dinners for assorted persons suffering from Christmas, Thanksgiving, or Easter depression, you can slowly build up your own peer and extended-kin networks. That doesn't mean hanging around singles bars, either. Follow the advice that my mother always gave me about meeting "nice boys": Join a church. Join a political club—Democratic or Republican. It's true what they say about clubs: they need people to stuff envelopes, ring doorbells, make telephone calls, and write publicity releases. Churches always need workers. Develop hobbies, outside interests of any and all types. But these interests must mean involvement and contact with other people. Going to the theater or movies alone or with a friend really doesn't imply a high level of social interaction. Brief and shoddy contacts in a singles bar can be ego-shattering and not worth the psychological damage.

While this really seems like pretty low-level, Pollyanna advice, this is what a competent therapist would tell a lonely, depressed man or woman. Not all lonely people are depressed. Not all people who value solitude are lonely. Not all suicides are the result of loneliness or depression. A lot are. All of us have frail emotions. We live in a frantic, mad world. Coping is a difficult task. Sometimes an impossible one. The pangs of a rainy Sunday afternoon all alone are momentary. Too many lonely rainy Sunday afternoons and the depression becomes ingrained.

Happy, healthy egos do not appear full-blown and can often suddenly disappear in the wake of a divorce or an unwanted job transfer. We all have to work hard every day to maintain reasonably functioning egos. While getting out of bed every day is a coping mechanism and a commitment to life, getting through the rest of the day can be traumatic. Stupid, silly incidents often prove a trigger to depression or repressed anger. Last spring, I wandered around in a blue funk for two days when the Post Office increased its first-class rate from thirteen to fifteen cents. The week before, I had carefully and prudently bought a sheet of thirteen-cent stamps so that I would not have to scrounge around my desk drawers frantically searching for a stamp to mail a letter. The thought of buying a sheet of two-cent stamps to match my useless thirteen-cent stamps was simply too much. I muttered and growled for two days, "The world is crazy. Not me, the world is crazy. Nothing works. I can't stand it." I did withstand this crisis. And come to think of it, I never did buy the sheet of two-cent stamps. Recognizing life's difficulties and those danger signals—in ourselves and our friends—we may survive much better.

11

Stress and Coping

Where Are We Now?

CONTRARY to the authors of most how-to books, I give you a *caveat*. There ain't no free lunch. In essence, all the books, all the theories, all the research come up to a grandiose zero. The theories are in a state of confusion. The research is indefinite. The studies are contradictory. We are going to do the best with what we've got.

Acute physiological stress produces psychological symptoms. The psychological symptoms, in turn, produce manifest and debilitating results: coronary, ulcer, arthritis, menstrual problems, mental illness, etc. That much we do know. The personality variables that enable one person to cope with stress while another cannot—this is where the confusion lies.

Once again we see the constant philosophical argument between Hobbes and Locke. As you undoubtedly remember from your beginning philosophy courses, Hobbes believed that man was basically a nasty brute who answered only to primeval needs. Man (or woman) really was a basically biological creature with a very thin veneer of civilization. In times of stress, that veneer gets stripped away and the beast pops out. On the other hand, Locke thought that man was basically a good, rational, *human* being. The humanness of mankind is that, no matter what the situation, man seeks to improve himself and seeks a greater good for mankind as a whole. This raging fight continues in psychology, psychiatry, industrial management, industrial psychiatry, and basic social psychology. Psychotherapy and self-help programs center on whether you are controlling your basic, inner impulses or whether as a rational human person you can reach a greater and better good.

I belong in the behavioral-modification, self-improvement, man-is-a-good-person camp. If we provide people with adequate-enough tools and the method for understanding, they can indeed control their own lives and perhaps, from the depths of understanding, scale the heights of happiness.

If You Don't Like It, Change It!

Here's where the list-making technique enters once again. Make lists of the things that you like to do, lists of the things you don't like to do, lists of the things that don't bug you, lists of the things that you absolutely, positively, and definitely cannot stand. Maybe make the lists on three or four separate pieces of paper, line them up on your dining-room table, and take a long, hard look at them. What bugs you about yourself? What bothers you about other people? What is it about your job that you cannot stand? What do you want to change?

One of the basic philosophical tenets of North American United States society lies in the Protestant ethic. Success. Striving. Need achievement. Upward social mobility. Here is the ingredient of our very cultural ethos. These are all the things that "they" said to Americans:

- You can't build a bridge here.
- You won't win the war.
- You can't become the president of the company.
- Blacks don't belong here.
- Women can't go to college.
- You can't drain the swamp.
- You can't send a man to the moon.

The American answer to all of the above statements was, "Phooey!" Basic American strength itself and what we call a "can-do" philosophy still prevail. Self-doubt, self-appraisal, self-analysis, and tragic introspection belong to the 1960s. There are solutions for everything. There isn't just one answer. There may be several answers. There are a series of viable alternatives open to every human being.

Thus the motto "If you don't like it, change it!" Take another look at that series of lists that you made. What are the things on that list over which you do have some kind of control? If your nose is too big, find yourself a good cosmetic surgeon and a couple of thousand dollars. If your hips are too wide, go on a diet and start an exercise program. If you hate your job, take some advance courses and get another job. If you don't like your commuting, move in closer or find yourself a car pool. Stop bitching and start rearranging. Once again, however, we must interject a note of caution: Those very things you use as a crutch and a complaint really don't matter at all. For example, what happens when you have thought for years or told yourself and your friends for many years that the reason that people don't like you is because you have a big nose? You go to the cosmetic surgeon and get a tiny, upturned, perky little nose—and people still don't like you. Now you are in big trouble. You have to decide whether or not you or your nose is to blame. Unfortunately, the general conclusion probably will have to be with YOU. Then what to do?

More Lists

Now we have to decide what happens to you when you are under stress. What things go on when you really can't cope. Or you're coping through a physiological reaction. Are these some of your symptoms?

- Insomnia.
- Tingling of the hands or feet.
- Excessive sleep.
- Stomach pains.
- Squeezing pains in the chest.
- Shortness of breath.
- Headaches.
- Migraine headaches.

- Diarrhea.
- Constipation.
- Menstrual disorders.
- False pregnancy.
- Problems conceiving.
- You name it and you've got it.

All right, you have the classic physiological symptoms of stress, combined with some of the classic depression symptoms. Where to go and what to do? Your body is giving you a message. Are you ready to interpret the message?

Coping Mechanisms

You have the message. You've accepted the underlying agenda. How, then, do you cope with stress? One of the best ways, of course, is complete withdrawal. You may compartmentalize—that is, pretend the problem doesn't exist. That's the old head-in-the-sand routine. It will go away. It really doesn't exist. Unfortunately, your problems do exist and you have to deal with them.

So, if withdrawal isn't an adequate method to reduce your stress, you can remove it. If your job is too much, quit or get another job. If your family obligations are overwhelming, divide up the work among the children and your spouse (if you have one). If you can't do that, find yourself some sort of household help, as we discussed in a previous chapter. Having your mother move in with you may be a source of stress in one way, but at least it can take some of the physical work load off your shoulders. Baby-sitting pools, car pools, room and board for a graduate student, an *au pair* girl who wants to learn English—these are means by which you can survive. Mutual exploitation is called co-operation these days.

Other lists may tell you to scale down your expectations. Do your lists tell you that you want to write the great American novel? Well, the initial question here is, do you have the talent and the time to do it? I have many friends who are artists who don't paint, sculptors who don't sculpt, writers who don't write, and singers who barely can carry a tune. Fantasy life is good on the bus on the way home or to dream the night away. When fantasy starts to impinge on reality, you've got problems. Someone other than your mother or your great-aunt really must tell you if your paintings are good or bad. How much sacrifice are you willing to make for creativity? Are you using your so-called unused talent as a club to induce guilt in your family?

How many wives—academic, military, and corporate—blame their husbands with the song of "if I hadn't married you, I would have. . . ." The "would have" ranges from writing the great American novel to finding a cure for cancer. These women would not have succeeded. They know it. Nonetheless, they like to pretend that these great and wonderful things would accrue to them had they not played the great martyr role in devoting themselves to their husbands' career and family development. Nonsense!

Once again, we see the "can do" philosophy at work in my simplistic explanation. If you want to do it and you have reasonable time constraints, you can do it. A friend of mine wrote a novel night after night until three o'clock in the morning. It got published and was a minor success. She wasn't content with being a minor success, but at least she got the book published. Another friend of mine has pittered and pattered about with her paints for years, has had several mild successes, and is content. That's probably the thing that most of us have to learn in our lives: that we will be *mild* successes. The true, honest-to-God Hemingways and Picassos are few and far between.

But have fun. Why not? Fun is missing from our lives. Fun is a coping mechanism. Having dinner out. Taking a weekend off. A trip away. Or just simply an afternoon downtown shopping all by yourself. Unfortunately, the Protestant ethic tells us that we can't have fun in our never-ending search for success. Therein lies the strain of ulcers and heart attacks. You need fun, humor, friends, strength, and joy.

Support System

Probably the most important method of coping is to develop your own personal and reasonably satisfying support system. What is it the old song tells us? "Everybody Needs Somebody." Data on suicide rates show us that. The unmarried (single, widowed, divorced) kill themselves at a faster rate than the married. Married people with children kill themselves at a lesser rate than married people without children. These grim realities bring home the fact that when you have someone to talk to and share your problems with, the difficulties are reduced in size. If you don't have a spouse, parent, or children old enough to share your concerns, you had better start building your own personal network. In an age in which one out of every five families in the United States move at least once during the year and families move at least an average of every four years, geographical mobility contributes to our loneliness and sense of anomie (normlessness). Rootless and unhappy, we move from place to place, losing whatever sense of continuity we ever did have.

Don't laugh at Welcome Wagon; it fulfills some very serious needs. If you are church- or synagogue-inclined, join not only for the Sunday-morning activities but for whatever else—children, adults, choir, reading, introspection, or study—that it can offer to you. If you have kids (or you don't), Boy Scouts, Girl Scouts, brownies, or cubs can help fulfill your unfulfilled maternal needs or help you integrate yourself with your own children. Divorced? A single parent? Parents Without Partners helps solve single-parent-loneliness problems. Alcoholics Anonymous. Gamblers Anonymous. Groups joined together to help prevent drug abuse. Wives and children of alcoholics. Golden-age clubs. All of the aforementioned provide a sense of belonging for people who desperately need those social contacts.

Don't sneer at any of these. The ones who sneer or sniff the loudest are probably those who need these very clubs and networks the most. In the past ten years, women's groups themselves have provided reasonably healthy psychological outlets for young and not-so-young women seeking to find their place within a male world. Some of these women's groups still are in the consciousness-raising stage of the 1960s. Most have advanced beyond that, however. Find yourself a group of reasonably like-minded women. You can start your own consciousness-raising group or join up with some of the more established groups. These may include NOW (National Organization for Women) or WEAL (Women's Equity Action League). All you have to do is look in your local yellow pages or telephone book to find these two large organizations. Once again, your church or synagogue may even have a women's group. The BPW (Business and Professional Women) and the AAUW (American Association of University Women) have changed their faces dramatically in the past few years, as has also the League of Women Voters. These traditionally hidebound women's organizations are now marching to the tune of a different drummer. Practically all of them are action-oriented. They are concerned with women fulfilling themselves and women dealing with women's problems in a man's world. Women are taking over new male management and supervisory roles. Heretofore, the best a woman could ever have hoped to be would be the supervisor in the typing pool. Another role she might possibly have fulfilled would be the super-duper administrative assistant. She wielded power and sometimes had a high salary. That was all. Women are moving into the board room and into the vice-presidential and presidential offices. They are even moving into the Pentagon as deputy under secretaries and under secretaries of defense. They have gone to the military academies. Yale and Harvard have long since been stormed. What happens to these new M.B.A.'s and Ph.D.'s?

Well, many of them are getting ulcers. A large proportion of them cannot seem to reconcile the traditional role with that of aggressive, hard-nosed, hard-driving supervisors. Man's best friend is not his dog but, rather, the faithful secretary who keeps bringing him coffee. How often can you be expected to withstand the continual and constant barbs of your jealous male colleagues? They are jealous because you have risen faster than they. The reason you rise so fast is because of equal-opportunity legislation and not brains. Perhaps new management styles are in order.

Masculinity + Femininity = Androgyny

Remember the discussion about old concepts of masculinity and femininity and the new idea of androgyny? The person who is high in "good masculine" and "good feminine" characteristics is reasonably well rounded. The person who is high in caring and high in competition is best suited for the executive board room and the corporation suite. "Bad masculine" characteristics, such as "cruel, ruthless, vicious, implacable" don't help you in your rise to the top, and "bad feminine" characteristics such as "passive, overly emotional, unstable, and unreliable" won't get you anywhere.

But a reasonably unflappable person who enjoys both masculine and feminine interests, who is not afraid to be open with her emotions, who is considerate of subordinates and interested in the personal and professional lives of those people around her—she will be a good manager, a good supervisor, and can be trusted with the key to the executive ladies' washroom. At the same time, the woman manager learns that she does not have to adopt a complete set of masculine mannerisms or even dress. Being a beautiful, well-groomed woman with an active sex life and well-balanced home life and a large paycheck is possible.

Women graduates now realize that they do not have to make either-or decisions: either be a happy wife or a successful lawyer. Other women have decided that they have neither time nor energy to devote to both family and career, so they will scale down their career aspirations for a while. Others have kinetic energy to spare, happy households, gourmet-cook housekeepers, beautifully behaved children, and adoring husbands. Mazel tov! To them will go the spoils. But, divorced, single, married, babied, or childrened—these women are coping.

There is a silent revolution going on and many women are coping extremely well. A part of the "greening" or the more "humane" part of the managerial ethic these days is the helping, coping, understanding supervisor who contributes to the psychic and psychological well-being of subordinates. The job gets done and done well. Employee peer groups work in tandem in a participative manner to reach a group goal. The good supervisor is sensitive to the needs and aspirations of the work group as a whole. While the kind of task determines the pace of the work group, most managerial principles are built on this competitive/nurturant/competent dimension. Psychologically it is androgynous behavior, but common-sense stereotypes still refer to these "caring" attributes as "feminine."

Women are better equipped sociologically to fill the managerial roles. That is not to say that there are not some—or many—ruthless, calculating, egomaniacal females in the business world. I predict that they won't last. These women—like the worst kind of men, whom they emulate—will fall in the corporate battle. The Herzberg-Maslow-Lewinian concepts of managerial leadership and supervisory style involve the kind and caring person.

Men are at a decided disadvantage, because they must learn to unfreeze their emotions. It is to be hoped that there are many androgynous and caring men around, just as there seem to be an untapped reservoir of androgynous women. But large corporations demand rigid adherence to bureaucratic ideals or the company ethic. The person who rises to the top does so at the risk of failing suddenly at the upper levels.

Who Rises to the Top?

More and more women are entering middle management, and a few are getting scattered through the upper echelons as well. The same kind of behavior holds true, male or female. The rise to the top is generally by conforming to top management and corporate ideals. The person who keeps her mouth shut, shows some administrative skills, has a reasonably balanced personality, and can get a job done well and efficiently *probably* will make it. There is no doubt that in these days of equal opportunity and the Department of Justice sniffing through personnel records, there has been an active search for women and minorities to fill slots that were previously closed to them. By legal fiat, fear of a lawsuit, sheer ability, or sexual wiles, the women are there. Then disaster, more often than not, strikes. It strikes women, minorities, and white males with about the same frequency. A person rises to the top by conforming. Once at the upper level, he or she must do a 180° turn and become a creative, independent thinker. Of course, this again depends on the corporation. There are some organizations, such as publishing companies and research-and-development consultant firms, that require nothing but independence and creativity. But let's talk about our ordinary, everyday, hierarchically organized corporation. Susy or Sammy Corporation Climber must now behave in an entirely different manner. The question is whether or not the person is adaptable enough to maintain his or her vice-presidential slot. Thus it is not surprising that most companies have to, at the upper level, engage in some kind of charm school and management training for their new young executives. Those behaviors that get you to the top won't keep you there. Or maybe they will.

The people-oriented/high-relationship-and-task-oriented (androgynous) personality will make it. In the era of the all-volunteer Army, for example, military men (and women) are fast learning that the people-oriented leader is more effective than the authoritarian one. Young men and women in large corporations want more from their jobs than simply money. Self-fulfillment is the byword. They demand some kind of respect, prestige, and a personal relationship both with the corporation and their supervisors. Women—not naturally but through their peculiar socialization—are thus better equipped for these new management/leadership roles. What is tough, lean, and *macho* is no longer effective.

Being the lone woman supervisor or the highest-ranking woman in a corporation is stress-producing itself. While some women may have the mental ability to be effective supervisors, the strain of being the sole female role model may reduce their effectiveness. Also, a woman's work role combined with that of wife and mother with no surcease or relief from these roles is a dual and often triple burden.

Time Management

What are the secrets and tricks of the trade that allow wives and mothers, lovers, to be high-ranking executives? The tricks range from eating lots of casseroles to having a full-time gourmet cook installed in the kitchen. Standards of cleanliness are really not too high. Working wife/mother cannot afford the luxury of a guilty conscience. When your son fails grade-four arithmetic, it neither means that you are a bad mother nor that the kid will end up a rapist. Both those possibilities may belong to the full-time stay-at-home mother as well.

But, grade-four arithmetic notwithstanding, most mothers figure out how they can survive. My own children became gourmet cooks at a very early age. They learned the one easy rule in the household, which was, "If you want to eat it, you had better learn how to cook it." At age five the baby became an accomplished pastry cook. I earned F's from the other, stay-at-home mothers but managed somehow to maintain my own sanity.

Healthy Mind and Body

Yet sanity is not only a question of time management for women executives but, like male executives, the combination of a healthy mind and a healthy body. Coronary, hypertension, high cholesterol levels, and cardiovascular problems are linked to a lack of exercise. Housewife and executive, we are a sedentary people. Kenneth Cooper aerobics and jogging have led to the current masses of people jogging and jiggling throughout suburban, urban, and even rural areas. If it isn't jogging, we had better start in on tennis, Yoga, swimming, or going to our favorite spa. Mind over body. Mind and body. Good exercise and good psychological mind-set.

If you're the kind of person who thinks about exercise more than doing it, this kind of sermon is almost self-defeating. But facts are facts and we simply cannot ignore that hypertension is a serious problem among middle management and upper executives in this society. Frequent vacations, changes of scene, good rest, nutritious food, cutting down on cigarettes, drinking moderately are all the sermons that have been preached to you by your own private physician and health magazines for years.

Whatever Works

What a strange, long journey in this book! From new concepts of masculinity and femininity to diets, suicide rates, and alcoholism, to jogging. So be it. If you can find relief in this crazy world, and still function—your solution is worthwhile. Est. Transactional analysis. Primal scream. Rosey Grier and needlework. The balanced Roman *media via* is hard to find in a world of commuter tie-ups and crazy production schedules.

In spite of all the brouhaha in all the literature and in spite of the rising ulcer rates and divorce rates, women executives seem to be coping. Some of them may be coping better than their male counterparts. The feminine perspective is a humane perspective. Caring, loving, being sympathetic to another person's feelings, and respecting another person's ethnic background or religion are eminently worthwhile traits. If these are "feminine" traits, then the feminine point of view is valuable. Maybe we can rescue psychological sanity and sociological imagination from the statistical tables and the computer printouts. Perhaps we can get rid of much social-science jargon by remembering that most languages other than English give gender to every noun.

"Love" in Spanish is a masculine word. "Dignity" is feminine. Love and dignity. Male and female. That adds up to "human." That's what social science is supposed to be all about.

BIBLIOGRAPHY

1 WHAT IS STRESS?

Astin, Helen S.; Parelman, Allison; and Fisher, Anne. *Sex Roles: A Research Bibliography*. National Institute of Mental Health, HEW Publication No. ADM 7437. Washington, D.C.: U. S. Government Printing Office, 1974.

Bowman, G. W.; Worthy, N. B.; and Greyser, S. A. "Are Women Executives People?" *Harvard Business Review* 43, July–August 1965:14–30+.

Dickman, Donna McCord. "Noise and Its Effect on Human Health and Welfare," *Ear, Nose & Throat Journal* 56, January 1977: 38–46.

Guthrie, George M.; Verstraete, Anne; Deines, Melissa M.; and Stern, Robert M. "Symptoms of Stress in Four Societies," *The Journal of Social Psychology* 95 (1975), 165–72.

Hollon, Charles J.; and Gemmell, Gary R. "A Comparison of Female and Male Professors on Participation in Decision Making, Job Related Tension, Job Involvement, and Job Satisfaction," *Educational Administration Quarterly* 12(2) (Winter 1976), 90–93.

Holmes, T. H.; and Rahe, R. H. "The Social Readjustment Rating Scale," *Journal of Psychosomatic Research* 11 (1967), 213–18.

Miller, James D. "Effects of Noise on People," *Acoustical Society of America* 56(3) (September 1974), 729–64.

Miller, Jean Baker, M.D.; and Mothner, Ira. "Psychological Consequences of Sexual Inequality," *American Journal of Orthopsychiatry* 41(5) (October 1971), 767–75.

Selye, Hans. *The Stress of Life*. New York: McGraw-Hill, 1956, revised 1976.

——. "Forty Years of Stress Research: Principal Remaining Problems and Misconceptions," *CMA Journal* (Canadian Medical Association journal), July 3, 1976, 115:53–56.

Sheehy, Gail. *Passages: Predictable Crises of Adult Life*. New York: E. P. Dutton, 1976.

Statistical Bulletin October 1972. "Rise in Accidental Deaths Among Women."

Thomas, Caroline Bedell; and Duszynski, Karen R. "Closeness to Parents and the Family Constellation in a Prospective Study of Five Disease States: Suicide, Mental Illness, Malignant Tumor, Hypertension and Coronary Heart Disease," *Johns Hopkins Medical Journal* B4, May 1974:251–70.

Uhlenhuth, Eberhard, M.D.; Lipman, Ronald S.; Balter, Mitchell B.; and Stern, Martin. "Symptom Intensity and Life Stress in the City," *Arch. Gen. Psychiatry* 31, December 1974:759–64.

Welford, A. T. "Stress and Performance," *Economics* 16(5), 1973:567–80.

Wittkower, E. D.; and Warnes, H. "Transcultural Psychosomatics." In *Mechanisms in Symptom Formation*, Proc. 2nd Congr. Int. College Psychosom. Med., Amsterdam 1973 (1974), 1–12.

2 THE UNIQUE CASE: WEST POINT

Lever, Janet; and Schwarts, Pepper. *Women at Yale: Liberating a College Campus*. Indianapolis: Bobbs-Merrill, 1975.

Peterson, J. A.; and Kowal, D. M. "Project 60: A Comparison of Two Types of Physical Training Programs on the Performance of 16–18 Year Old Women." West Point, N.Y.: Office of Physical Education, 1977.

Priest, R. F.; and Houston, J. W. "Analysis of Spontaneous Cadet Comments on the Admission of Women." West Point, N.Y.: Office of the Director of Institutional Research, Report 76-014, May 1976.

Priest, R. F. "Cadet Attitudes Toward Women 1975." West Point, N.Y.: Office of the Director of Institutional Research, Report 76-015, May 1976.

———. "A Comparison of Faculty and Cadet Attitudes Toward Women." West Point, N.Y.: Office of the Director of Institutional Research, Report 76-017, May 1976.

———. "Changes in Cadet Attitudes Toward the Admission of Women to West Point." West Point, N.Y.: Office of the Director of Institutional Research, Report 76-018, June 1976.

———. "The Effect of Company and CBT Testing Day on New Cadet Attitudes, Class of 1980." West Point, N.Y.: Office of the Director of Institutional Research, Report 7T-008, September 1976.

———. "Who Are the West Point Cadets?" Paper presented at the

1976 Regional Meeting of the Inter-University Seminar on Armed Forces and Society, Air Command and Staff College, Maxwell AFB, Alabama, October 1976.

———; Prince, H. T.; Rhone, T.; and Vitters, A. G. "Differences Between Characteristics of Men and Women New Cadets Class of 1980." West Point, N.Y.: Office of the Director of Institutional Research, Report 77-010, March 1977.

Priest, R. F. "Cadet Perceptions of Inequitable Treatment During Cadet Basic Training 1976." West Point, N.Y.: Office of the Director of Institutional Research, Report 77-012, March 1977.

———; and Houston, J. W. "New Cadets and Other College Freshmen, Class of 1980." West Point, N.Y.: Office of the Director of Institutional Research, Report 77-013, March 1977.

Priest, R. F. "The Intergroup Contact Hypothesis as Applied to Women at West Point." West Point, N.Y.: Office of the Director of Institutional Research, Report 77-015, June 1977.

Stauffer, R. "Comparison of United States Military Academy Men and Women on Selected Physical Performance Measures . . . Project Summertime." West Point, N.Y.: Office of Physical Education, October 1976.

Vitters, A. G.; and Kinzer, N. S. "Preliminary Report on Women Cadets at the United States Military Academy." Paper presented at the 1976 Regional Meeting of the Inter-University Seminar on Armed Forces and Society, Air Command and Staff College, Maxwell AFB, Alabama, October 1976.

———. *Report of the Admission of Women to the U. S. Military Academy (Project Athena).* Department of Behavioral Sciences and Leadership, United States Military Academy. West Point, N.Y., September 2, 1977.

———; and Priest, Robert F. "Women at West Point: A Case Study in Organizational and Interpersonal Change." Paper prepared for delivery at the 1977 Inter-University Seminar National Biennial Conference, October 20–22, 1977, Chicago, Ill.

Vitters, Alan G.; and Kinzer, Nora Scott. "Women at West Point: Change Within Tradition." *Military Review,* April 1978: 20–28.

United States Military Academy. "Project 60A." West Point, N.Y.: Department of Tactics, 1976.

3 WOMEN ABROAD

Astin, Helen S.; Parelman, Allison; and Fisher, Anne. *Sex Roles:*

A Research Bibliography. Rockville, Md.: National Institute of Mental Health, U. S. Department of Health, Education and Welfare, 1975.

Blumberg, Rae Lesser. "Fairy Tales and Facts: Economy, Family, Fertility, and the Female." In I. Tinker and M. Bo Bramsen. *Women and World Development.* Washington, D.C.: Overseas Development Council, 1976:12–21.

Bucinic, Mayra. *Women and World Development; An Annotated Bibliography.* Washington, D.C.: Overseas Development Council, 1976.

Chaney, Elsa. "Women in Politics in Latin America: The Case of Peru and Chile." In Ann Pescatello (ed.). *Female and Male in Latin America.* Pittsburgh: University of Pittsburgh Press, 1973:103–39.

———. "Old and New Feminists in Latin America: The Case of Peru and Chile," *Journal of Marriage and the Family* 35(2), 1973:331–43.

Cohen, Lucy M. *Las Colombianas ante la Renovación Universitaria.* Bogotá: Tercer Mundo, 1971.

———. "Woman's Entry to the Professions in Colombia: Selected Characteristics," *Journal of Marriage and the Family* 35(2), 1973:322–30.

Elu de Leñero, María del Carmen. *Perspectivas femininas en América Latina.* Mexico, D.F.: Sep Setentas, 1976.

Jaquette, Jane. "Literary images and female role stereotypes: the woman and the novel in Latin America." In Ann Pescatello (ed.). *Female and Male in Latin America.* Pittsburgh: University of Pittsburgh Press, 1973:3–27.

———. "Women in Revolutionary Movements in Latin America," *Journal of Marriage and the Family* 35(2), 1973:344–54.

Kinzer, Nora Scott. "Women Professionals in Buenos Aires." In Ann Pescatello (ed.). *Female and Male in Latin America.* Pittsburgh: University of Pittsburgh Press, 1973:159–90.

———. "Priests, Machos and Babies: or, Latin American Women and the Manichaean Heresy." In *Journal of Marriage and the Family* 35(2) (May 1973), 300–12.

———. "Sexist Sociology," *The Center Magazine,* May/June 1974: 48–59.

———. "Sociocultural Factors Mitigating Role Conflict in Buenos Aires Professional Women." In Ruby Rohrlich-Leavitt. *Women Cross-Culturally; Change and Challenge.* The Hague: Mouton Press, 1975:181–97.

———. "Destruyendo el mito: la porteña profesional." In María del

Carmen Elu de Leñero (ed.). *Perspectivas femininas en América Latina*. Mexico, D.F.: Sep Setentas, 1976:83–100.

Knaster, Meri. "Women in Latin America: The State of Research," *Latin American Research Review* XI(1), 1975:3–74.

Luiggi, Alice H. 65 *Valiants*. Gainesville, Fla.: University of Florida Press, 1965.

Pescatello, Ann. *Female and Male in Latin America*. Pittsburgh: University of Pittsburgh Press, 1973.

Rohrlich-Leavitt, Ruby. *Women Cross-Culturally; Change and Challenge*. The Hague: Mouton, 1975.

Saffioti, H. I. "Female Labor and Capitalism in the United States and Brazil." In R. Rohrlich-Leavitt. *Women Cross-Culturally; Change and Challenge*. The Hague: Mouton, 1975:59–94.

Stevens, Evelyn P. "The Prospects for a Woman's Liberation Movement in Latin America," *Journal of Marriage and the Family* 35(2), 1973:313–21.

——. "Marianismo: the other face of *Machismo* in Latin America." In Ann Pescatello (ed.). *Female and Male in Latin America*. Pittsburgh: University of Pittsburgh Press, 1973:89–101.

——. "Machismo and Marianismo," *Society* 10(6) Sept.–Oct. 1973:57–63.

Stycos, J. Mayone. *Ideology, Faith, and Family Planning in Latin America; Studies in Public and Private Opinion on Fertility Control*. New York: McGraw-Hill, 1971.

Tinker, Irene; and Bo Bramsen, Michele. *Women and World Development*. Washington, D.C.: Overseas Development Council, 1976.

4   WOMEN AND THE NEW MANAGEMENT STYLES

Argyris, Chris. *Integrating the Individual and the Organization*. New York: John Wiley, 1964.

——. *Interpersonal Competence and Organizational Effectiveness*. Homewood, Ill.: Irwin-Dorsey, 1962.

——. *Personality and Organization*. New York: Harper & Row, 1957.

Bardwick, Judith. *Readings on the Psychology of Women*. New York: Harper & Row, 1972.

Bem, S. L. "The measurement of psychological androgyny," *Journal of Consulting and Clinical Psychology* 42 (1974), 155–62.

——. "Sex-role adaptability: One consequence of psychological androgyny," *Journal of Personality and Social Psychology* 31 (1975), 634–43.

———. "Fluffy Women and Chesty Men," *Psychology Today*, Sept. 1975:58–62.

———. "On the utility of alternate procedures for assessing psychological androgyny," *Journal of Consulting and Clinical Psychology* 45 (1977), 196–205.

———; and Lenney, E. "Sex-typing and the avoidance of cross-sex behavior," *Journal of Personality and Social Psychology* 33 (1976), 48–54.

Bem, S. L.; Martyna, W.; and Watson, C. "Sex typing and androgyny: Further explorations of the expressive domain," *Journal of Personality and Social Psychology* 34 (1976), 1016–1023.

Bernard, Jessie. "The Paradox of the Happy Marriage." In V. Gornick and B. K. Moran (eds.). *Woman in Sexist Society. Studies in Power and Powerlessness*. New York: Mentor Books, 1971:145–62.

———. *Women and the Public Interest; An Essay on Policy and Protest*. New York: Aldine, 1971.

———. "Change and Stability in Sex-Role Norms and Behavior," *Journal of Social Issues* 32(3), 1976:207–23.

Blake, Robert R.; and Mouton, Jane S. *Corporate Excellence Through Grid Organization Development*. Houston, Tex.: Gulf Publishing Co., 1968.

———. *The Managerial Grid*. Houston, Tex.: Gulf Publishing Co., 1964.

Bond, J. R.; and Vinacke, W. E. "Coalitions in Mixed-sex Triads," *Sociometry* 21 (1961), 61–75.

Bowman, G. W.; Worthy, N. B.; and Greyser, S. A. "Are Women Executives People?" *Harvard Business Review* 43, July–August 1965:14–30.

Bradford, Leland P.; Gibb, Jack R.; and Benne, Kenneth D. (eds.). *T-Group Theory and Laboratory Method*. New York: John Wiley, 1964.

Broverman, Inge; Broverman, D.; Clarkson, Frank E.; Rosenkrantz, P. S.; and Vogel, S. R. "Sex-Role Stereotypes and Clinical Judgments of Mental Health," *Journal of Consulting and Clinical Psychology* 34(1), 1970:1–7.

Cartwright, Dorwin; and Zander, Alvin (eds.). *Group Dynamics Research and Theory*. New York: Harper & Row, 1968, 3rd ed.

Chafetz, Janet Saltzman. *Masculine/Feminine or Human? An*

Overview of the Sociology of Sex Roles. Itasca, Ill.: F. E. Peacock, 1974.

Chapman, J. Brad; and Luthans, Fred. "The Female Leadership Dilemma," *Public Personnel Management,* 4(3) (May–June 1975), 173–79.

Condry, John; and Dyer, Sharon. "Fear of Success: Attribution of Cause to the Victim," *The Journal of Social Issues,* 32(3), 1976:63–83.

Drucker, Peter. *The Effective Executive.* New York: Harper & Row, 1967.

Dubin, Robert. *Human Relations in Administration.* Englewood Cliffs, N.J.: Prentice-Hall, 1961.

Friedan, Betty. *The Feminine Mystique.* New York: Dell, 1963.

——. *It Changed My Life. Writings on the Women's Movement.* New York: Dell, 1976.

Gardner, Burleigh B.; and Moore, David G. *Human Relations in Industry.* Homewood, Ill.: Irwin, 1964.

Gardner, John. *Self-Renewal: The Individual and the Innovative Society.* New York: Harper & Row, 1964.

Gornick, Vivian; and Moran, Barbara K. *Woman in Sexist Society. Studies in Power and Powerlessness.* New York: Mentor Books, 1971.

Haire, Mason. *Psychology in Management.* New York: McGraw-Hill, 1956.

—— (ed.). *Modern Organization Theory.* New York: John Wiley, 1959.

——. *Organization Theory in Industrial Practice.* New York: John Wiley, 1962.

Herzberg, Frederick. *Work and the Nature of Man.* Cleveland, Ohio: World, 1966.

——; Mausner, Bernard; and Snyderman, Barbara. *The Motivation to Work.* New York: John Wiley, 1959, 2nd ed.

Horner, Matina S. "Toward an understanding of achievement-related conflicts in women," *Journal of Social Issues* 28(2), 1972:157–76.

Kanter, Rosabeth Moss. *Men and Women of the Corporation.* New York: Basic Books, 1977.

Katz, Daniel; and Kahn, Robert L. *The Social Psychology of Organizations.* New York: John Wiley, 1966.

Kinzer, Nora Scott. "Women Professionals in Buenos Aires." In Ann Pescatello (ed.). *Female and Male in Latin America.* Pittsburgh, Pa.: University of Pittsburgh Press, 1973.

——. "Soapy Sin in the Afternoon," *Psychology Today,* August 1973.

——. "Class War Under the Hair Dryer," *Psychology Today*, April 1974.

——. "The Beauty Cult," *The Center Magazine*, November 1974.

——. "Beast in the Beauty Salon," *The Saturday Evening Post*, December 1974.

——. "Sociocultural Factors Mitigating Role Conflict in Buenos Aires Professional Women." In Ruby R. Leavitt (ed.). *Women Cross-Culturally: Change and Challenge*. The Hague: Mouton, 1975.

Leavitt, Harold J. *Managerial Psychology*. Chicago: University of Chicago Press, 1964, 2nd ed.

——; and Pondy, Louis R. (eds.). *Readings in Managerial Psychology*. Chicago: University of Chicago Press, 1965.

Levinson, Harry. *Emotional Health in the World of Work*. New York: Harper & Row, 1964.

——. *The Exceptional Executive*. Cambridge, Mass.: Harvard University Press, 1968.

Levinson, Harry; and Price, Charlton R. *Men, Management, and Mental Health*. Cambridge, Mass.: Harvard University Press, 1962.

Lewin, Kurt. *A Dynamic Theory of Personality*. New York: McGraw-Hill, 1945.

——. *Field Theory in Social Science: Selected Theoretical Papers*. New York: Harper & Row, 1951 (paperback).

Likert, Rensis. *New Patterns of Management*. New York: McGraw-Hill, 1961.

——. *The Human Organization*. New York: McGraw-Hill, 1967.

——; and Hayes, Samuel P., Jr. (eds.). *Some Applications of Behavioral Research*. New York: UNESCO, 1957.

Maslow, Abraham H. *Eupsychian Management: A Journal*. Homewood, Ill.: Irwin-Dorsey, 1965.

——. *Motivation and Personality*. New York: Harper & Row, 1954.

——. *Toward a Psychology of Being*. Princeton, N.J.: D. Van Nostrand, 1968, 2nd ed.

Mayo, Elton. *Human Problems of an Industrial Civilization*. Cambridge, Mass.: Harvard University Press, 1933.

McClelland, David C.; et al. *The Achievement Motive*. New York: Appleton-Century-Crofts, 1953.

McClelland, David C.; and Winter, David J. *Motivating Economic Achievement*. New York: The Free Press, 1969.

McGregor, Douglas. *The Human Side of Enterprise*. New York: McGraw-Hill, 1960.

——. *Leadership and Motivation*. Edited by W. G. Bennis, and

E. H. Schien, with Caroline McGregor. Cambridge, Mass.: M.I.T. Press, 1966.

——. *The Professional Manager*. Edited by Caroline McGregor and W. G. Bennis. New York: McGraw-Hill, 1967.

Menninger, William G.; and Levinson, Harry. *Human Understanding in Industry: A Guide for Supervisors*. Chicago: Science Research Associates, 1956.

Millman, Marcia; and Kanter, Rosabeth. *Another Voice; Feminist Perspectives on Social Life and Social Science*. New York: Anchor Books, 1975.

Murphy, Gardner. *Personality: A Biosocial Approach to Origins and Structure*. New York: Basic Books, 1966.

Neff, Walter S. *Work and Human Behavior*. New York: Atherton Press, 1968.

Odiorne, George S. *Management by Objectives*. New York: Pitman, 1965.

Osborn, Richard; and Vicars, William M. "Sex Stereotypes: An Artifact in Leader Behavior and Subordinate Satisfaction Analysis?" *Academy of Management Journal* 19(3), 1976:439–49.

Roby, Pamela. "Sociology and Women in Working-class Jobs." In M. Millman and R. Kanter (eds.). *Another Voice; Feminist Perspectives on Social Life and Social Science*. New York: Anchor Books, 1975, 203–39.

Roethlisberger, F. J.; and Dickson, William J. *Counseling in an Organization: A Sequel to the Hawthorne Research*. Boston: Harvard University Graduate School of Business, 1966.

——. *Management and the Worker*. Cambridge, Mass.: Harvard University Press, 1939.

Rosenkrantz, Paul; Vogel, S.; Bee, H.; Broverman, Inge; and Broverman, D. M. "Sex-Role Stereotypes and Self-Concepts in College Students," *Journal of Consulting and Clinical Psychology* 32(3), 1968:287–95.

Rossi, Alice S. "Barriers to the Career Choice of Engineering, Medicine, or Science Among American Women." In Jacquelyn A. Mattfeld and Carol G. Van Aken. *Women and the Scientific Professions*. Cambridge, Mass.: M.I.T. Press, 1965.

Rush, Harold M. F. *Behavioral Science Concepts and Management Application*. New York: National Industrial Conference Board, 1969.

Schein, Edgar H. *Organizational Psychology*. Englewood Cliffs, N.J.: Prentice-Hall, 1965.

——; and Bennis, Warren G. *Personal and Organizational Change Through Group Methods.* New York: John Wiley, 1965.

Schein, Virginia E. "The Woman Industrial Psychologist: Illusion or Reality?" *American Psychologist* 26(8) (August 1971), 708–12.

Spence, Janet. "Thematic Apperception Test and Attitudes Towards Achievement in Women: A New Look at the Motive to Avoid Success and a New Method of Measurement," *Journal of Counseling and Clinical Psychology* 42 (June 1974), 427–37.

——. "Ratings of Self and Peers on Sex-Role Attributes and Their Relation to Self-Esteem and Conceptions of Masculinity and Femininity," *Personality and Social Psychology* 32 (July 1975), 29–39.

——; Helmreich, R.; and Stapp, J. "The Personal Attributes Questionnaire: A Measure of Sex-Role Stereotypes and Masculinity and Femininity," *Journal of Supplement Abstract Service, Catalog of Selected Documents Psychology* 4 (1974), 43.

Spence, Janet; and Helmreich, Robert. *Masculinity and Femininity. Their Psychological Dimensions, Correlates and Antecedents.* Austin, Tex.: University of Texas Press, 1978.

Spencer, Bradford F.; and Gress, Jearald R. "Successful Behaviors Which Breed Failure," *U-M (University of Michigan) Business Review* 26 (November 1974), 6–9.

Vroom, Victor H. *Work and Motivation.* New York: John Wiley, 1964.

Whyte, William F. *Man and Organization: Three Problems in Human Relations in Industry.* Homewood, Ill.: Irwin, 1959.

Willett, Roslyn S. "Working in a 'Man's World': The Woman Executive." In V. Gornick and B. K. Moran (eds.). *Woman in Sexist Society. Studies in Power and Powerlessness.* New York: Mentor Books, 1971, 511–32.

5 STRESS, HEALTH, AND DISEASE

Cannon, W. B. *The Wisdom of the Body.* New York: W. W. Norton, 1932.

Friedmann, M.; and Rosenman, R. W. *Type A Behavior and Your Heart.* New York: Alfred A. Knopf, 1974.

Grant, I.; Kyle, G. C.; Teichman, A.; and Mendels, J. "Recent Life Events and Diabetes in Adults," *Psychosomatic Medicine* 36(2) (March–April 1974), 121–27.

Henryk-Gutt, Rita; and Rees, W. Linford. "Psychological Aspects of Migraine," *Journal of Psychosomatic Research* 17, 1973:141–53.

Holden, Constance. "Cancer and the Mind: How Are They Connected?" *Science* (June 23, 1978), 1363–69.

Holme, Ingar; Froili, Aksel; and Leren, Paul. "Mental Stress and Coronary Rise Factors, The Oslo Study," *Journal of Oslo City Hospital* 27(1) (Jan. 1977), 3–7.

Hurst, Michael W.; Jenkins, C. David; and Rose, Robert M. "The Relation of Psychological Stress to Onset of Medical Illness," *Annual Review of Medicine* 27 (1976), 301–12.

Katz, J. L.; Weiner, Herbert; Gallagher, T. F.; and Helman, Leon. "Stress, Distress, and Ego Defenses: Psychoendocrine Response to Impending Breast Tumor Biopsy," *Archives of General Psychiatry* 23, Aug. 1970:131–42.

Muslin, Hyman L.; Gyarfas, Kalman; and Pieper, William J. "Separation Experience and Cancer of the Breast," *Annals New York Academy of Sciences* 125 (1966), 802–6.

Paloucek, Frank P.; and Graham, John B. "The Influence of Psycho-Social Factors on the Prognosis in Cancer of the Cervix," *Annals New York Academy of Sciences* 125 (1966), 814–16.

Paull, Andrew; and Hislop, Ian G. "Etiologic Factors in Ulcerative Colitis: Birth, Death and Symbolic Equivalents," *International Journal of Psychiatry in Medicine* 5(1), 1974:57–64.

Rees, W. Linford. "Personality and Psychodynamic Mechanisms in Migraine," *Mechanisms in Symptom Formation*, Proc. 2nd Congr. Int. College Psychosom. Med., Amsterdam 1973, 23 (1974), 111–22.

Silen, William. "Stress Ulcers," *Medical Trial Technique Quarterly* 20 (1974), 254–66.

Solomon, George F.; Amkraut, Alfred A.; and Kasper, Phyllis. "Immunity, Emotions and Stress," *Mechanisms in Symptom Formation*, Proc. 2nd Congr. Int. College Psychosom. Med., Amsterdam 1973, 23 (1974), 209–17.

Surawicz, Frida G. "Women, Cancer and Emotions," *Journal of the American Medical Women's Association*, 32(1) (Jan. 1977), 18–27.

Thomas, Clayton L. "Special Problems of the Female Athlete." In Allan J. Ryan and Fred L. Allman, Jr. (eds.). *Sports Medicine.* New York: Academic Press, 1974, 347–73.

Wolff, H. G. *Stress and Disease.* Springfield, Ill.: Charles C Thomas, 1968.

6 STRESS, MARRIAGE, AND CHILDREN

Berger, B. M.; Hackett, B. H.; and Millar, R. M. "Child Rearing in Communes." In L. K. Howe (ed.). *The Future of the Family.* New York: Simon & Schuster, 1972.

Bernard, Jessie. "Development Tasks of the NCFR-1963-1988," *Journal of Marriage and the Family* 26 (1964), 29–38.

——. "Present Demographic Trends and Structural Outcomes in Family Life Today." In J. A. Peterson (ed.). *Marriage and Family Counseling, Perspective and Prospect.* New York: Association Press, 1968.

——. *The Future Of Marriage.* New York: World, 1972. (Paper ed., New York: Bantam, 1973.)

Blumberg, Rae Lesser. "From Liberation to Laundry: A Structural Interpretation of the Retreat from Sexual Equality in the Israeli Kibbutz," paper presented at the American Political Science Association, Chicago, 1974.

Friedan, B. *The Feminine Mystique.* New York: W. W. Norton, 1963.

Glick, P. C. "Dissolution of Marriage by Divorce and Its Demographic Consequences." Liege, Belgium: International Population Conference, 1973.

——; and Norton, A. J. "Perspectives on the Recent Upturn in Divorce and Remarriage," *Demography* 10 (1973), 301–14.

Gorsuch, Richard; and Key, Martha K. "Abnormalities of Pregnancy as a Function of Anxiety and Life Stress," *Psychosomatic Medicine* 36(4) (July–August 1974), 352–62.

Hartley, R. "American Core Culture: Changes and Continuities." In G. H. Seward and R. C. Williamson (eds.). *Sex Roles in Changing Society.* New York: Random House, 1970.

Helsen, R. "The Changing Image of the Career Woman," *Journal of Social Issues* 28 (1972), 33–46.

Hoffman, Saul. "Marital Instability and the Economic Status of Women," *Demography* 14(1) (February 1977), 67–76.

May, Robert R. "Mood Shifts and the Menstrual Cycle," *Journal of Psychosomatic Research* 20 (1976), 125–30.

Pearlin, Leonard I. "Status Inequality and Stress in Marriage," *American Sociological Review* 1975 40, June:344–57.

Seiden, Anne M. "Overview: Research on the Psychology of Women I. Gender Differences and Sexual and Reproductive

Life," *American Journal of Psychiatry* 133(9) (September 1976), 995–1007.

Seidenberg, Robert. *Corporate Wives—Corporate Casualties?* Garden City, N.Y.: Anchor, 1975.

Terman, L. M. *Psychological Factors in Marital Happiness.* New York: McGraw-Hill, 1938.

7   STRESS AND FEMALE PLUMBING

"Abortion," *Newsweek*, June 5, 1978, 37–47.

Aguiar, R. "The Effects of the Menstrual Cycle in Heterosexual Relationships," *Marriage and Family Counselors Quarterly* 11(1), 1976:11–25.

Bart, Pauline. "Depression in middle-aged women." In V. Gornick and B. K. Moran (eds.). *Woman in Sexist Society: Studies in Power and Powerlessness.* New York: Basic Books, 1971, 163–86.

Berger, Lawrence R. "Abortions in America: The Effects of Restrictive Funding," *New England Journal of Medicine* 298(26) (June 29, 1978), 1474–77.

Bernard, Jessie. *The Future of Motherhood.* New York: Dial Press, 1974. (Paper ed. Baltimore: Penguin Books, 1975.)

——. "Adolescence and Socialization for Motherhood." In S. E. Dragistin and G. H. Elder, Jr. (eds.). *Adolescence in the Life Cycle; Psychological Change and Social Context.* New York: Halsted Press, 1975, 227–52.

Brecher, Jeremy. "Sex, Stress, and Health," *International Journal of Health Services* 7(1), 1977:89–101.

Corea, Gena. *Women's Health Care: The Hidden Malpractice.* New York: William Morrow, 1977.

De Marchi, W. G. "Psychophysiological Aspects of the Menstrual Cycle," *Journal of Psychosomatic Research* (Oxford) 20(4), 1976:279–87.

Donelson, Elaine; and Gullahorn, Jeanne E. *Women: A Psychological Perspective.* New York: John Wiley, 1977.

Everett, Royice B.; and Schecter, Marshall D. "A Comparative Study of Prenatal Anxiety in the Unwed Mother," *Child Psychiatry and Human Development* 2(2) (Winter 1971), 84–91.

Farrell, Barbara L.; and Allen, Margaret F. "Physiologic/Psychologic Changes Reported by USAF Female Flight Nurses During Flying Duties," *Nursing Research* 22(1) (January–February 1973), 31–36.

Fleischauer, Mary L. "A Modified Lamaze Approach in the Treatment of Primary Dysmenorrhea," *Journal of the American College Health Association* 25(4), 1977:273–75.

Golub, Sharon. "The Magnitude of Premenstrual Anxiety and Depression," *Psychosomatic Medicine* 38(1), 1976:4–12.

Gorsuch, Richard L.; and Key, Martha K. "Abnormalities of Pregnancy as a Function of Anxiety and Life Stress," *Psychosomatic Medicine* 36(4) (July–August 1974), 352–62.

Harper, Juliet; and Williams, Sara. "Early Environmental Stress and Infantile Autism," *The Medical Journal of Australia*, 1974:341–46.

Institute of Medicine. *Legalized Abortion and the Public Health.* Washington, D.C.: National Academy of Sciences, 1975.

Kessler, Judith Ann. *Marital Interaction, Social Networks, and the Menstrual Cycle.* Unpublished Ph.D. dissertation, University of Notre Dame, 1976.

Koeske, Randi Daimon. "Premenstrual emotionality: is biology destiny?" *Women and Health* 1(3), 1976:11–14.

Lane, Ellen A. "The Sex Ratio of Children Born to Schizophrenics and a Theory of Stress," *The Psychological Record* 19 (1969), 579–84.

Levy, Judith M.; and McGee, Richard K. "Childbirth as Crisis: A Test of Janis's Theory of Communication and Stress Resolution," *Journal of Personality and Social Psychology* 1975 31(1), 171–79.

Marinari, Kathleen T.; Leshner, Alan; and Doyle, Maureen. "Menstrual Cycle Status and Adrenocortical Reactivity to Psychological Stress," *Psychoneuroendocrinology* (Oxford), 1(3), 1976:213–18.

May, Robert R. "Mood Shifts and the Menstrual Cycle," *Journal of Psychosomatic Research* (Oxford), 20(2), 1976:125–30.

McBride, A. B. *The Growth and Development of Mothers.* New York: Harper & Row, 1973.

McCoy, Norma L. "Innate Factors in Sex Differences," *Nursing Forum* 15(3), 1976, 277–93.

Peck, E. *The Baby Trap.* New York: Pinnacle Books, 1972.

Pollitt, John. "Symptoms of Stress: Part 1—Types of Stress and Types of People," *Nursing Mirror* (London), 144(24), 1977, 13–14.

———. "Sex Difference and the Mind," *Proceedings of the Royal Society of Medicine* (London), 70(3), 1977, 145–48.

President's Commission on Population Growth and the American Future. *Population and the American Future.* New York: Signet Books, 1972.

Seiden, Anne M. "Overview: research on the psychology of women. I. Gender differences and sexual and reproductive life," *American Journal of Psychiatry* 133(9), 1976:995–1007.

Snow, Loudell F.; and Johnson, Shirley M. "Modern Day Menstrual Folklore: Some Clinical Implications," *Journal of the American Medical Association,* 237(25), 1977:2736–39.

Tubbs, Walter; and Carnahan, Clarence. "Clinical Biofeedback for Primary Dysmenorrhea: A Pilot Study," *Biofeedback and Self-Regulation* 1(3), 1976, 323.

Tylden, Elizabeth. "Hyperemesis and Physiological Vomiting," *Journal of Psychosomatic Research* 12 (1968), 85–93.

van Keep, Pieter A.; and Kellerhals, Jean M. "The Impact of Socio-Cultural Factors on Symptom Formation: Some Results of a Study of Ageing Women in Switzerland," *Mechanisms in Symptom Formation,* Proc. 2nd Congr. Int. College Psychosom. Med., Amsterdam 1973, Psychother. Psychosom. 23 (1974), 251–63.

Venables, Peter H.; and Christie, Margaret J. *Research in Psychophysiology.* New York: John Wiley, 1975.

Weyland, Carol June. *Primary Dysmenorrhea and Its Relation to Sexual Attitudes.* Unpublished Ph.D. dissertation, Catholic University of America, 1976.

Weideger, Paula. *Menstruation and Menopause: The Physiology and Psychology, the Myth and the Reality.* New York: Alfred A. Knopf, 1975 (rev. 1977).

Zaharieva, Ekaterina. "Olympic Participation by Women: Effects on Pregnancy and Childbirth," *Journal of the American Medical Association* 221(9) (August 28, 1972), 992–95.

8 STRESS, DRUGS, ALCOHOL, AND FOOD

Abelson, Herbert I.; Fishburn, Patricia M.; and Cisin, Ira. *National Survey on Drug Abuse: 1977. A Nationwide Study—Youth, Young Adults and Older People. Vol. 1 Main Findings.* Washington, D.C.: National Institute on Drug Abuse, U. S. Department of Health, Education, and Welfare, 1977.

Allon, Natalie. *Group Dieting Interaction.* Unpublished Ph.D. dissertation, Brandeis University, 1972.

Beckman, L. J. "Women Alcoholics: A Review of Social and Psychological Studies," *Journal of Studies in Alcoholism* 36(7) (July 1975), 797–824.

Cahalan, Don; and Cisin, Ira H. "American Drinking Practices: Summary of Findings from a National Probability Sample. II. Measurement of Massed Versus Spaced Drinking," *Quarterly Journal of Studies on Alcohol* 29(3) (September 1968), 632–56.

Cooper, James R. *Sedative-Hypnotic Drugs: Risks and Benefits.* Washington, D.C.: National Institute on Drug Abuse, U. S. Department of Health, Education, and Welfare, 1977.

Corrigan, Eileen M. "Women and Problem Drinking: Notes on Beliefs and Facts," *Addictive Diseases: An International Journal* 1(2), 1974:215–22.

Edwards, G.; Henseman, C.; and Petro, J. "A Comparison of Female and Male Motivation for Drinking," *Journal of Intentional Addictions* 8(4), 1973:577–87.

Hoffman, H. Jackson. "Differential Personality Inventory for Male and Female Alcoholics," *Psychological Reports* 34(1) (February 1974), 21–22.

Jolliffe, Norman (ed.). *Clinical Nutrition.* New York: Harper & Row, 1962.

Knupfer, G.; and Room, R. "Drinking Patterns and Attitudes of Irish, Jewish and White Protestant American Men," *Quarterly Journal of Studies on Alcohol* 28(4) (December 1967), 676–99.

Lawrence, Joseph J.; and Maxwell, Milton A. "Drinking and Socio-Economic Status." In D. Pittman and R. Snyder (eds.). *Society, Culture, and Drinking Patterns.* Carbondale, Ill.: Southern Illinois University Press, 1962, 141–45.

Lindbeck, Vera L. "The Woman Alcoholic: A Review of the Literature," *The International Journal of the Addictions* 7(3), 1972, 567–80.

Miller, Peter M.; Hersen, Michel; Eisler, Richard M.; and Hilsman, Gray. "Effects of Social Stress on Operant Drinking of Alcoholics and Social Drinkers," *Behavior Research and Therapy* 12 (1974), 67–72.

Parker, Frederick B. "Sex-Role Adjustment in Women Alcoholics," *Quarterly Journal of Studies in Alcoholism* 33 (1972), 647–57.

Pittman, David; and Snyder, Charles R. *Society, Culture, and Drinking Patterns.* Carbondale, Ill.: Southern Illinois University Press, 1962.

Roe, Daphne A.; and Eickwort, Kathleen R. "Relationships Between Obesity and Associated Health Factors with Unemployment Among Low Income Women," *Journal of American Medical Women's Association* 31(5), 1976, 193–204.

Schuckit, Marc A.; and Gunderson, E. K. Eric. "Alcoholism in Navy and Marine Corps Women: A First Look," *Military Medicine* 140, April 1975:268–71.

Schmidt, Wolfgang; and de Lint, Jan. "Causes of Death of Alcoholics," *Quarterly Journal of Studies in Alcoholism* 33 (1972), 171–85.

Suburban Housewives and Alcohol, a study for the United Presbyterian Church in the U.S.A. North Conway Institute, 8 Newbury Street, Boston, Mass. 02116, December 1967.

Valentine, Nancy M. "Women and Alcoholism: A Bibliography," *JPN and Mental Health Services* 14(12) (December 1976), 23–27.

Wilsnack, S. C. "Femininity by the Bottle," *Psychology Today* 6(11) (April 1973), 39–43.

Wyden, Peter. *The Overweight Society*. New York: William Morrow, 1965.

9 STRESS AND MENTAL ILLNESS

Bart, Pauline. "Depression in Middle-Aged Women." In V. Gornick and B. K. Moran (eds.). *Woman in Sexist Society: Studies in Power and Powerlessness*. New York: Basic Books, 1971.

Bardwick, J. *Psychology of Women*. New York: Harper & Row, 1971.

Broverman, I. K.; Broverman, D. M.; Clarkson, F.; Rosenkrantz, P. S.; and Vogel, S. R. "Sex-Role Stereotypes and Clinical Judgments of Mental Health," *Journal of Consulting and Clinical Psychology* 34 (1970), 1–7.

Chesler, Phyllis. "Patient and Patriarch: Women in the Psycho-Therapeutic Relationship." In V. Gornick and B. K. Moran (eds.). *Woman in Sexist Society: Studies in Power and Powerlessness*. New York: Basic Books, 1971.

——. *Women and Madness*. New York: Doubleday, 1972.

French, John R. P.; and Caplan, Robert D. "Organizational Stress and Individual Strain," *Occupational Mental Health* 3(1), 1973:30–66.

Horney, K. *Feminine Psychology*. New York: W. W. Norton, 1973.

Maccoby, E. E.; and Jacklin, C. *The Psychology of Sex Differences*. Stanford, Calif.: Stanford University Press, 1974.

Pollitt, John. "Sex Difference and the Mind," *Proceedings of the Royal Society of Medicine* 70 (March 1977), 145–48.
Schless, Arthur P.; Teichman, Alicia; Mendels, J.; and DiGiacomo, J. N. "The Role of Stress as a Precipitating Factor of Psychiatric Illness," *British Journal of Psychiatry* 130 (1977), 19–22.
Schuckit, Marc A.; and Gunderson, E. K. Eric. "Psychiatric Incidence Rates for Navy Women: Implications for an All Volunteer Force," *Military Medicine* 139 (July 1974), 534–36.
Seiden, Anne M. "Overview: Research on the Psychology of Women. II. Women in Families, Work, and Psychotherapy," *American Journal of Psychiatry* 133(10) (October 1976), 1111–23.
Servan, George. "Relationship of Mental Status, Functioning and Stress to Readmission of Schizophrenics," *British Journal of Social and Clinical Psychology* 14 (1975), 291–301.
Williams, Juanita H. *Psychology of Women. Behavior in a Biosocial Context.* New York: W. W. Norton, 1977.

10 STRESS AND THE ULTIMATE SOLUTION: SUICIDE

Burvill, P. W. "Recent Decreased Ratio of Male : Female Suicide Rates, Analysis of Rates in Selected Countries, Specific for Age and Sex," *International Journal of Social Psychology* 18(2), 1972:137–39.
Durkheim, E. *Suicide.* Glencoe, Ill.: Free Press, 1951.
Gibbs, Jack P. (ed.). *Suicide.* New York: Harper & Row, 1968.
Henry, A. F.; and Short, V. F. *Suicide and Homicide: Some Economic, Sociological, and Psychological Aspects of Aggression.* New York: Free Press, 1964.
Iga, Mamoru; Yamamoto, Joe; and Noguchi, Thomas. "The Vulnerability of Young Japanese Women and Suicide," *Suicide* 5(4) (Winter 1975), 207–22.
Mausner, J. S.; and Steppacher, R. C. "Suicide in Professionals: A Study of Male and Female Psychologists," *American Journal of Epidemiology* 98(6), 1973:436–45.
Morris, Jeffrey B.; Kovacs, Maria; Beck, Aaron T.; and Wolffe, Andrew. "Notes Toward an Epidemiology of Urban Suicide," *Comprehensive Psychiatry* 15(5) (Nov.–Dec. 1974), 537–47.
Newman, John F.; Whittemore, Kenneth R.; and Newman, Helen G. "Women in the Labor Force and Suicide," *Social Problems* 21(2) (Fall 1973), 220–30.
Public Health Paper No. 58. *Prevention of Suicide.* Geneva: World Health Organization, 1974.

Sanborn, Donald E., III; Sanborn, Charlotte J.; Cimbolic, Peter; and Niswander, G. Donald. "Suicide and Stress-Related Dermatoses," *Diseases of the Nervous System* 33, June 1972:391–94.

Slettin, Ivan W.; Brown, Marjorie L.; Evenson, Richard C.; and Altman, Harold. "Suicide in Mental Hospital Patients," *Diseases of the Nervous System* 33, May 1972:328–34.

Southgate, M. Therese. "Remembrance of Things (Hopefully) Past (Suicide Among Physicians)," *Journal of the American Medical Association* 232(13) (June 30, 1975), 1331–32.

Steppacher, Robert C.; and Mausner, Judith S. "Suicide in Male and Female Physicians," *Journal of the American Medical Association* 228(3) (April 15, 1974), 323–28.

Yolles, Stanley. *Suicide: A Public Health Problem.* In H. L. P. Resnick (ed.). *Suicidal Behaviors.* New York: Little, Brown, 1968.

11 STRESS AND COPING

Bond, J. R.; and Vinacke, W. E. "Coalitions in Mixed-Sex Triads," *Sociometry* 21 (1961), 61–75.

Bowman, G. W.; Worthy, N. B.; and Greyser, S. A. "Are Women Executives People?" *Harvard Business Review* 43 (1965), 14–16+.

Dewar, Elaine. "The New Psychotherapies," *Maclean's Magazine,* April 1977:23–25.

Kanter, Rosabeth Moss. *Men and Women of the Corporation.* New York: Basic Books, 1977.

Kiev, A. A. *A Strategy for Handling Executive Stress.* Chicago, Ill.: Nelson-Hall, 1974.

Levinson, Harry. "On Being a Middle-Aged Manager," *Harvard Business Review* 49, July–August 1969:51–59.

———. *Executive Stress.* New York: Harper & Row, 1970.

Maccoby, Michael. *The Gamesman.* New York: Simon & Schuster, 1976.

Mechanic, D. *Students Under Stress. A Study in the Social Psychology of Adaptation.* Glencoe, Ill.: Free Press, 1962.

Odiorne, George S. "Executives Under Siege: Strategies for Survival," *Management Review* 67, April 1978:7–12.

Orth, Charles D., III. "How to Survive the Mid-Career Crisis," *Business Horizons* 17(5) (October 1974), 11–18.

Page, R. C. *How to Lick Executive Stress.* New York: Simon & Schuster, 1966.

Reif, William W.; Newstrom, John W.; and St. Louis, Robert D., Jr. "Sex as a Discriminating Variable in Organizational Reward Decisions," *Academy of Management Journal* 19(3), 1976:469–76.

Saint-Clair, Simone. *Ravensbrück, L'Enfer des Femmes.* Paris: Fayard, 1945.

———; and Monestier, Marianne. *58 Actions Héroïques de la Résistance.* Paris: Grund, 1971.

Schein, Virginia E. "The Relationship Between Sex Role Stereotypes and Requisite Management Characteristics," *Journal of Applied Psychology* 57(2), 1973:95–100.

Selye, Hans. *Stress Without Distress.* New York: Signet Books, 1974.

Spence, Janet. "Ratings of Self and Peers on Sex-Role Attributes and Their Relation to Self-Esteem and Conceptions of Masculinity and Femininity," *Personality and Social Psychology* 32, July 1975:29–39.

———. "Thematic Apperception Test and Attitudes Towards Achievement in Women: A New Look at the Motive to Avoid Success and a New Method of Measurement," *Journal of Consulting and Clinical Psychology* 42, June 1974:427–37.

———; Helmreich, R.; and Stapp, J. "The Personal Attributes Questionnaire: A Measure of Sex-Role Stereotypes and Masculinity and Femininity," *Journal of Supplement Abstract Service, Catalog of Selected Documents in Psychology* 4 (1974), 43.

Tillion, Germaine. *Ravensbrück.* Garden City, N.Y.: Anchor Press, 1975.

Toffler, A. *Future Shock.* New York: Random House, 1970.

Wilson, William P. "Mental Health Benefits of Religious Salvation," *Diseases of the Nervous System* 33, June 1972:382–86.

INDEX

Abortion, 148–50
Absenteeism, job, 118
Addiction, 153–77
  alcoholism, 155–59
  dependency relationship,
    171–72
  diet pills, 173–75
  drugs, 160–67
  food, 167–71
  remedies for, 175–77
Adrenal glands, 8
Adrenocorticotropic hormone
  (ACTH), 8
Agoraphobia, 186
Aggression, 11, 52, 53, 65, 67
Agitated depression, 207–8
Al-Anon, 176
Alcohol and alcoholism, 11, 24,
    25, 79, 160, 167, 200, 222
  pills combined with, 5
  use of, 153–55
  women and, 155–59
Alcoholics Anonymous, 156–59,
    167, 172, 176, 198, 234
Alka Seltzer, 13
Amenorrhea, 138
American Association of Uni-

versity Women (AAUW),
  235
American Broadcasting Com-
  pany (ABC), 42
American College Testing Pro-
  gram, 37
American Medical Association,
  135
American Sociological Associa-
  tion, 200
Androgynous personality, 65
Androgyny, 76, 236–38
  among men, 78–80
Angst, 19
Anomic suicide, 205, 214–18,
  222
Anomie, 19
Antabuse, 158
Anxiety, 4, 92, 94, 123, 143,
  145, 147
Argentina, women in, 55–58
Armstrong, Ann, 108
Assembly (magazine), 34–35
Athena (goddess), 28

Barbiturates, 161
Bart, Pauline, 151–52